THE DRUIDS

Uncovers the mysterious world of the
Druids, their religious beliefs and
practices, and their impact on history
and the literary imagination.

Also in this series:

ALCHEMY: The Great Work
Cherry Gilchrist
DRACULA: The Novel and the Legend
Clive Leatherdale
FAIRY TALES: Allegories of the Inner Life
J. C. Cooper
THE GOLDEN DAWN: Twilight of the Magicians
R. A. Gilbert
MYSTICISM: The Direct Experience of God
Michael Cox
PYTHAGORAS: Lover of Wisdom
Ward Rutherford
SYMBOLISM: The Universal Language
J. C. Cooper

THE DRUIDS

Magicians of the West

by

WARD RUTHERFORD

THE AQUARIAN PRESS
Wellingborough, Northamptonshire

First published 1978
First Trade Paperback Edition 1983
Second Impression 1984

British Library Cataloguing in Publication Data

Rutherford, Ward
    The Druids.
    1. Druids and Druidism—History
    I. Title
    299'.1'6   BL910

    ISBN 0-85030-346-X

*The Aquarian Press is part of the
Thorsons Publishing Group*

Printed and bound in Great Britain

Contents

Esoteric Themes and Perspectives Series

The aim of this wide-ranging series is to provide a comprehensive library of background information and contextual insights for those interested in the history and development of esoteric thought.

Preface

THE Druids are old acquaintances, partly perhaps because I am a Jerseyman, that is to say, I come from what was once part of Gaul, most extensive of the Celtic domains, and like all of them, strongly conscious of its past.

It was, at any rate, as a schoolboy in Jersey that I was first introduced to them by the great island historian, George Balleine. He was a man who approached his subject, even when it involved his own locality, with a proper scepticism and he believed that much accepted about the Druids, including the then widely held belief that they had been the builders of Stonehenge, was nonsense. A great deal, in his view, had to be both learnt and unlearnt.

It was, in fact, just this mystery and uncertainty surrounding them which most fascinated me. But when I tried to satisfy my curiosity about them I soon discovered just how impenetrable these qualities were. The only complete work on the subject, Kendrick's, was principally concerned with debunking the received ideas of the time and, in so far as its author puts forward views of his own, they are extremely guarded and tentative. Outside of this were the various briefer references in books about the Gauls or the Celts generally.

Disappointed, I had to let the subject drop and the Druids would probably have remained for me one of those passing interests of adolescence, but for something which came many years later. In 1972 I wrote a book about a series of strange and terrifying sexual attacks which took place in Jersey over some fifteen years. When a perpetrator was brought to trial he claimed a black magic and witchcraft connexion going back to the Middle Ages. In trying to put the crimes into perspective I was compelled to re-examine these recurrent themes of island history and somewhat to my surprise I found myself driven back, willy nilly, through the past to the time of the Druids.

And it was thus that I made what was for me a most interesting double discovery. Not only is the practice of magic, "black" or "white", very closely associated with the Celtic lands, where it is still to be found, but in some unaccountable way it seemed to have left its mark on the nature of Christian belief within them. Why, for example, was the Protestant Reformation so complete in Brittany, Wales, Scotland, Northern Ireland, the Isle of Man and the Channel Islands? In Brittany, it is true, Catholicism later made good the losses it sustained at the hand of Huguenot Calvinism, though only by dint of massacre and repression and even then was forced to accept compromise. The Catholicism of Brittany is still acknowledged as possessing an individuality all its own and much the same can be said for that of Southern Ireland.

Could it be that something in Druidism, some attitude or cast of mind it developed in its adherents, had lingered to explain this?

Long afterwards the question nagged at me, but was not pursued. It would certainly have been pushed into some dusty pigeonhole of the mind, save for Gilles Cremonesi who suggested that there might actually be a book in it. At first I demurred. I am not a Celtic scholar, a comparative religionist or an archaeologist. It was Gilles who persuaded me that I was at least a practising historian.

It was, therefore, as an historian that I embarked on this book. Having first read the by now appreciable literature on the Druids, I went back to the primary sources — the references to them among the classical writers who could be called contemporary, and the Welsh and Irish mythologies with their strongly pagan Celtic ethos.

I also remembered that in Jersey are to be found a number of customs and beliefs to which pagan, in some cases expressly Druidic, origins are ascribed. I wondered whether something similar existed elsewhere and whether the Druidic link was anything more than romantic legend.

Soon I was overwhelmed by the sheer bulk of evidence and by the manifest similarities between local customs, beliefs and festivals found all over the Celtic world, and known Druidic practice. I am aware that mine has been a mere scratching of the surface. Professor Anne Ross, who has made far more intensive studies, has discovered an even greater number, and it is no exaggeration to say that one could devote an entire book to this single topic. It is something which must be taken account of, if only as a sign of the persistence, perhaps not of the Druids, but of Druidic ideas.

So, too, I came to realize must something else. From very early times the Druids were given parity with other, so-called "barbarian" religions in places infinitely remote from one another — in India, Persia and Babylon, now Iraq. Accordingly, in studying the Druids I very quickly found myself in the midst of what must have been a very broad band of religious beliefs, whose widely varying outward appearance often concealed astonishing deeper resemblances which, of course, I am not the first to have noticed.

We know that from earliest times down to our own, attitudes towards the Druids have been ambivalent. On the one hand are those who see them as nothing but the ministers of a crudely primitive even brutal crypto-religion, pandering to superstition and the lowest human instincts through overtly sexual "fertility rites" and human sacrifice. On the other, are the inflated claims made on their behalf to phenomenal and unsurpassed knowledge.

In trying to drive a mean course between these opposites, I think it fair to say I was as clear of preconceptions as a writer can be. I was far too intimidated by my subject and my own deficiencies in tackling it, to entertain them. My attitude towards magic, witchcraft and the paranormal is, to say the least, sceptical.

I think it important to make these preliminary observations so that the value or otherwise of my conclusions can be assessed. They were certainly not arrived at by prior design; they took me entirely by surprise.

I would particularly like to thank those people who gave me such unstinting and patient help, among whom were Colin Wilson; Geoffrey Ashe; Margaret Killip of the Manx Museum and National Trust; as well as two old friends, Joan Stevens of the Société Jersiaise and, among the august body's membership, Eileen Watkins. I would especially like to record my gratitude to my wife for the time and trouble she took going through this manuscript at a time when she had so many other cares and concerns.

I would also like to thank the following for allowing me to use photographs: the British Tourist Authority; the Department of Leisure and Tourist Services of Bath City Council; the Wales Tourist Board; the National Museum of Ireland; Gloucester City Museum and Art Gallery; Carlisle Museum and Art Gallery; the Editor of the *Oxford Times*; and in London the most helpful picture librarians of the National Tourist Organisation of Greece and the French Government Tourist Office.

CHAPTER ONE

The Ceaseless Quest

THE age we live in is, as we are constantly being told in varied tones of approval or disapproval, an areligious one. At best, religion is a cultural curiosity. The old fixities, whether of Heaven or Olympus, to which our acts, public or private, are referable, have become irrelevant.

We may well congratulate ourselves on our release from bigotry and superstition, but we ought also to recognize that for practical purposes we have reduced to two the criteria by which we can test our situation: the scientific, or as we might call it, the evolutionary one; and the occult or revelatory one, that of the astrologers, Theosophists, Rosicrucians, Tantrists, modern witches and their like.

Between these poles we are compelled to make a choice, without hope of compromise, for they tend in precisely contrary directions.

The evolutionary view is of a human race moving, however painfully and falteringly, towards greater knowledge and to an ever improved adaptation to environment as a result. Although few scientists might be prepared to put it so bluntly, their very activity posits the acceptance of something like Teilhard de Chardin's "Omega Point" towards which all knowledge converges and which will be reached at some time in an infinitely remote and hypothetical evolutionary future.

To the "revelationists" on the other hand, it is not the future but the past which is the key. It is that equally far distant moment at which the repository of knowledge — the "Ancient Wisdom" in Geoffrey Ashe's terminology — was entrusted to mankind. The future is merely taking us further away from it and, in consequence, adding to losses already incurred. So whereas the evolutionists believe in a progress from "primitive man", ignorant, superstitious, disorganized, in a word, poorly adapted, the revelationists see a retrogression from the time when all was known and understood. At best, they would say, what men have been scraping together amid so much anguish is an inadequate substitute for the genuine article. Worse, its very acquisition has tended to darken and sully the fountains of primal instinctual wisdom.

One scarcely need point out the inherent fallacies of their position: why, for example, was so little of this knowledge committed to some transmissible form? It is no sort of argument to claim it was, through, say, inscriptions on the walls of Egyptian tombs. On the revelationists' own tacit admission these are expressed in codes so obscure no two people seem agreed on their decipherment. Neither do any of the interpretations so far offered add anything startlingly new or likely to offer hopeful alternatives to the human race.

But the scientists cannot have it all their own way either. Their view of man leads all too quickly to a picture of his past existence which is false, misleading and arrogant. "Primitive man", like "Proto-man", is a pure construct with no demonstrable basis in reality. Pre-history totally fails to reveal beings strikingly less intelligent than ourselves. It simply shows that they proceeded from different premises and there is as little justification for supposing these entirely erroneous as for supposing our own entirely right. As a philosopher friend never tires of telling me, the very concept of evolution is one shot through with logical difficulties.

Worse still, scientists as a group suffer from a stubborn refusal to accept any limits to their methodology and a consequent refusal to consider possibilities which might upset accepted tenets. A notorious example is the field of so-called paranormal activity. On the whole, science has simply shunned it. Where it has deigned to apply tests, their negative results have been used to discredit the entire range of what, in fact, are totally unrelated phenomena.

It may well be that, as its advocates have always argued, this is a sphere in which reconstruction and quantifiability are impossible. There is not the slightest reason why, because one woman's dream of an air-crash happens to come hideously true, every such dream must do so or even why the same woman's subsequent dreams have all to be realized. The validity of the original experience is by no means impugned thereby. And in the one area where testing has proved possible, that of telepathy, the results have tended to support its existence. For all this, science's attitude has remained ambivalent where it has not been openly hostile. One thinks of the learned member of the French Academy of Sciences who, hearing Edison's phonograph for the first time, attempted to assault the inventor, accusing him of ventriloquism! It was unthinkable that a waxed cylinder could accommodate all the complex modulations of the human voice.

Such obduracy has been a polemical gift to the proponents of even the most esoteric forms of revelationist theory. They have been able to cash in on both the general, very reasonable feeling that "there are more things in heaven and earth, Horatio ..." and on the growing dissatisfaction with the sterilities of a materialism, at root that of the laboratory applied to human life. In response to these feelings they proffer their enticing range of alternatives which include even the quasi-scientific versions as exemplified by writers like Erich von Däniken, who tries to persuade us that the original bringers of knowledge were astronauts visiting earth. All these various schools promise, in the words of Evans-Wentz, "the coming of the Golden Age and enthronement of the Divine Wisdom on earth".

If, however, venerability is the criterion of respectability plainly it is the revelationists who have it. The post-Darwinian age is a bare century old, whereas when the Greek writer Hesiod, writing in the 8th Century BC, invented the term "Golden Age", he was merely giving title to a concept long accepted: that there had been some lost idyllic period in human history. In Judaism and hence in Christianity, it found expression in the story of the Garden of Eden, though, with a touch of Jewish realism, we are told that it was precisely through his efforts to acquire knowledge that Man lost his paradisaical state.

Thus the Classical world, too, contained those who were engaged in the search for a lost Ancient Wisdom. And it was not, they believed, to be found amid the complexities, the pressures, the corruptions and the luxuries of life in their own developed civilizations. Its inheritors must, therefore, exist in societies less polluted. So every encountered nation, and particularly those judged barbarian by Greek or Roman criteria, was scanned with the greatest care to see whether it was, indeed, The Inheritor.

It was obvious that Celtic society and its religion should have been an early subject for this. When Diviciacus, who may have been a Druid, visited Rome in 60 BC, educated Romans like Cicero hung on his words as though he were Plato reincarnate. In part, this was due to the amazement which so often seizes the expensively educated when they discover that those who have not enjoyed their advantages are not actually shuffling cretins. But in part, also, it was due to the longing to find a meaning to life.

Thereafter, and even at the very time the Roman legions were doing their ruthless utmost to annihilate them, the Druids were being extolled in some quarters on account of their knowledge and wisdom. Ostensibly, they vanished from human consciousness with the Roman conquest of Gaul and then Britain, though they undoubtedly survived in Ireland as well as in other places untouched or comparatively untouched by Roman influence up to the coming of Christianity, and in radically changed form perhaps after it. St Patrick is said to have discoursed with a pagan Celt who sounds like a Druid. St Columba denounced them in round terms, which makes it appear as if they existed to be an object for denunciation.

This was, nonetheless, the beginning of a period of obscurity in which the Druids were largely forgotten, certainly by the educated élite, and it lasted, more or less, until the Renaissance. In the 15th Century, however, the works of the classical authors once more became generally available and the references to the Celts and the Druids therein were grasped as casting a fresh, if fitful light, on pre-history. Apparently interest was lively enough to prompt Shakespeare to make actual Celtic kings the heroes of the two plays *Cymbeline* and *King Lear*.

There may have been a deeper reason for this sudden upsurge of interest in the past. This was the great age of explorations, rekindling old hopes, for Eldorado was always more than a purely materialistic dream. Consideration of the Indians of the New Colonies led logically to consideration of the native British as found by the Roman invaders and to the drawing of analogies. These were pressed to such lengths that in trying to convey an idea of what the Ancient Britons looked like illustrators drew freely on descriptions of the American Indians, even to feathered headdresses. And this inspired the beguiling theory that perhaps after all, the Golden Age and the Ancient Wisdom had actually coexisted in early Europe, even — if Caesar spoke truly — in Britain itself.

A further stimulus to this could have been Queen Elizabeth's Irish policies which brought her commissioners into intimate though hostile contact with the people and not only their myths but also those customs and institutions surviving from the distant past, such as the breed of wandering lawyers still to be found in the Ireland of the times. Though we cannot be sure that the link between Elizabethan Irish and pagan Celts was ever made, there was the definite dawning of an interest in Druidism. Michael Drayton in *Polyolbion* which appeared in 1622, declared the Druids to be sacred bards and philosophers second to none in their knowledge of "great Nature's depths", a view close to the classical idealization of them.

Over the subsequent centuries, the Druids were held up as the originators of metaphysical systems which grew ever more recondite and obscure with the years. Books on Celtic paganism and Druidism, possessing little more than a nodding acquaintance with the known facts proliferated and found an eager market. Within their pages bogus linguistics, the obscurities of the 6th Century Welsh poet Taliesin, the Druidic mistletoe rite and — with sad inevitability — the Scriptures, became utterly confused. Abraham and Noah found themselves become Druids, and patriarchal Judaism itself a British invention. Patriotism was scaling new heights.

It was the miseries and confusions of the Industrial Revolution which had given this fresh impetus to the chase back to the Druids for the Ancient Wisdom, and it is hardly surprising that he who so deplored "the dark, Satanic mills", the draughtsman-poet William Blake, should have been among those who hankered for a pagan past supposedly happier. He was introduced to it by one Owen Pughe, a man who helped to lead the vanguard of the movement which converted the Druids into the bearded Jehovahs most of us know.

But he was not alone. Eminent among the founders of this cult was the Lincolnshire physician and archaeological amateur, William Stukeley, who was one of the first to declare Stonehenge a Druidic monument, a fallacy which persists to our own times. Stukeley, who took Holy Orders, was less concerned with the Ancient Wisdom for itself, however, than with using the Druids to advance his own cause in the great theological debate of the day, that of "natural religion". Its thesis was that the worship of a deity was a natural human instinct and in support evidence was found from among primitive peoples. Stukeley was soon proving, to his own satisfaction, that Druidism and Christianity were virtually two sides of the same coin.

The links between Stonehenge and Druidism were further influenced, albeit indirectly, by the architect Inigo Jones, the man principally responsible for the introduction of the English Palladian style of building. Stuart Piggott points out that in his plan for the Circus at Bath, that showpiece of the genre, its designer, John Wood the Elder, may have been emulating the shape and proportions of Stonehenge. We know he believed Bath, the Roman *Aquae Sulis* and earlier the seat of the Celtic king Bladud, to have been the centre of a Celtic Apollonian cult (as it may well have been). He also believed the whole surrounding countryside, which includes Stonehenge, Wood Henge and Avebury Ring, to be the precise area to which the Druids must have come, since Caesar referred to their having originated in Britain. As it happened, the best available plan of Stonehenge at that time was one drawn up by Inigo Jones. This shows three entrances, facing roughly due south, due north and due north east, and corresponds very closely with the position of the three streets feeding into the Circus, which is also about the same size as the outer ditch and bank surrounding the standing stones.

The pursuit of the Ancient Wisdom, via a Celtic paganism and the Druids was not, however, to be satisfied solely by essays in archaeological speculation. Poets and composers with a desperate eye to the main chance came forward with outpourings alleged to be in the manner of the Celtic bards. There were even a few which were claimed as the genuine article, somehow miraculously preserved, to be discovered at this propitious moment.

Nor was the vogue confined by the English Channel. The French had made their own discovery of the Celts and found them to be highly desirable pre-Roman ancestors. When Pezron's *L'Antiquitez de la Nation et la Langue Celt* appeared in 1703 it was only the latest of a long line, but translated into English it was responsible for the introduction of the word "Celt" as an alternative to "Ancient Briton".

There was even a heavy tome published in France which claimed to be a codification of the Druidic legal system, and every chance archaeological find was immediately attributed to them, even when its provenance was plainly Roman or centuries later.

Italy which could justifiably claim a connexion with the Celts through Cisalpine Gaul soon joined in, to be followed by Germany, also with many Celtic links. Esaias Pufendorf's *Dissertatio de Druidibus* and *De Dis Germans* were high-flown titles for sensational works giving lurid descriptions of human sacrifice, the latter bearing a splendidly engraved frontispiece which incorporated a Druid with a blood-stained knife and what is presumably a Druidess playing a drum with a pair of human bones, while the background of a sacred grove is littered with corpses.

By this time, one's own megalith had become so *de rigueur* for every stately home-owner that the amenities of an estate which lacked one were considered pathetically inadequate. In a few cases, these had a real claim to antiquity. General Conway who as lieutenant-governor of Jersey in the early 19th Century had reorganized its fortifications against Napoleonic incursion was presented by the grateful islanders with one of the numerous dolmens to be found there. This was then crated up, shipped off and set up at his home at Henley-on-Thames where it has stood ever since. In those commoner cases where an original was unavailable, however, any circle of large stones stood duty.

Better still one might actually have a Druidic hermit in a cell attached to one's home. Visitors to the home of Rowland Hill, inventor of the Penny Post, were often frightened out of their wits by the bearded relic who suddenly revealed himself to them as they dallied innocently in the country-park.

It was inevitable that all this should sooner or later acquire institutional dignity in what one might call Druidic fan clubs. In October 1792, *The Gentleman's Magazine* reported the celebration of the autumn equinox by a group of Welsh expatriates in London who had set up a ring of stones on a site at Primrose Hill, with an altar or *Gorsedd* at its centre. The man behind this was a carpenter, Edward Williams, who had adopted the bardic pseudonym of Iolo Morganwg. Fascinated by all things Celtic and especially by the connexion with Wales, Williams had not scrupled to strengthen an exiguous case with forged documentary evidence.

There was, of course, not the slightest historical licence for the idea that the Druids had had stone altars. The classical descriptions, then the only available evidence, mention nothing of the kind (except for a figurative reference in Tacitus) and it can only have come about as a result of the equation between Druids and the megaliths. Nonetheless, in 1819, Williams set up his *Gorsedd* in the grounds of a Carmarthen hotel during the Eisteddfod there, using for the purpose stones taken from his pocket. Thereafter, bards and white robed Druids became insolubly linked with the Eisteddfod and have remained so. Dubious as their historical credentials may be, the organizers of the festival must feel a real debt of gratitude to Iolo, alias Williams, for providing them with the basis of the quaint and totally fanciful Druidic rituals which have become such a great tourist attraction.

But when it came to proving themselves true Celts, the Anglo-Saxons were not to be left behind by the Welsh. In the last two decades of the 18th Century, Druidic societies began to spring up all over England. One of the first of these, founded by another carpenter, Henry Hurle, was the Ancient Order of Druids. With its combination of esotericism and mutual assistance it was obviously intended to be something of a poor man's Freemasonry, but with the passage of time and a schism which divided it, it became a benefit society pure and simple and in this form has continued. In 1908, one of its branches, the Albion Lodge, at Oxford, gained an illustrious initiate in the person of Winston Churchill, though we have no record of his close involvement in its activities.

In 1872, the idea had spread to Germany, and the Druidic society formed there was affiliated to an International World Lodge of Druids.

It was all moving further and further from the pursuit of the Ancient Wisdom, though this degeneration did not pass without protest. The Order of the Golden Dawn, formed to try to bring mysticism back to the centre, included among its members the Irish poet W. B. Yeats.

The Order of Druids had already split on this very issue, losing those members who were primarily interested in things mystical. But the cabal they formed was soon itself riven by dissension, presumably over doctrine.

In 1915, Stonehenge was given to the nation by its then owner, Sir Cecil Chubb. Among those participating in the handing over ceremony were the members of a Druidic society. Soon afterwards no fewer than five such organizations were seeking permission to hold ceremonies on the site. By 1949, this number had dwindled to two. At the celebration of the summer solstice in 1955 only one appeared, the British Circle of the Universal Bond.

The sole claim to distinction this had was through its Chief Druid from 1909 to 1946: George Watson MacGregor Reid, a friend of George Bernard Shaw, had had the unusual distinction of standing for both the House of Commons and the American Senate and, incidentally, of failing to be elected to either. A magnificent bearded figure in keeping with the stereotype of the Druid, when his daughter died he cremated her remains on a funeral pyre in what he believed to be a re-enactment of Druidic ritual.

In 1963, the Circle of the Universal Bond lost a sizable proportion of its membership to the Order of Bards, Ovates and Druids, but the debunking of the idea that Stonehenge was built by Druids, which had begun with Kendrick in 1927, had now reached even these rarefied enclaves and could no longer be ignored. The site was deserted in favour of one at Tower Hill in London and another in Northampton.

But what of the quest for the Ancient Wisdom?

On this whole notion something more needs saying. As Geoffrey Ashe has so well demonstrated the idea has a peculiar persistence, and the assertion that there can be no knowledge outside that which humanity has so acquired by trial and error through the millennia of its evolution still begs too many questions.

It requires only a few moments' thought to realize that humanity possesses and takes for granted knowledge of an enormous number of things whose origins can hardly be ascribed to the workings of evolution as we understand and accept it. The discovery of fire and invention of the wheel are both attributed in most societies to supernatural intervention. Mystery surrounds the invention of decimal calculation and of writing. And what about astronomy, not only found world-wide, and throughout history, but also attributing the same kind of characteristics to the same planetary influences. The planet we know as Mars received its name because its influence was supposed to be responsible for wars, and hence the Romans, among others, gave it the name of their war god.

And what about the story of the Flood to be found in such diverse and widely separated mythologies as those of the Hebrews, the Babylonians, the Chinese and the South and Central American civilizations.

Or the dragon? A purely mythical creature who turns up with the same characteristics in India, China, Japan — and among the Celts. In a form perfectly recognizable to a Chinese it is, after all, the symbol of Wales.

Can we ascribe the laws of consanguinity, those seemingly fixed ordinances aimed at prohibiting incest and inbreeding to the ordinary work-ings of evolution? How, then does one account for their existence among cultures which have not even made the connexion between copulation and parturition? How could these ideas have been disseminated?

Then there is the interesting case of the Hebrew Kosher Laws, an extremely elaborate system of dietary and other rules of hygiene, pre-cisely designed for the needs of wandering peoples living in a torrid desert. The Bible quite specifically gives them a divine source. We can accept or reject this as we please, but can we on the other hand believe they evolved?

Of course, these are not reasons for rejecting evolutionary in favour of revelatory theory. But they do indicate other forces at work, forces perhaps not known to us, perhaps, one might say, part of a lost Ancient Wisdom?

Or might we?

CHAPTER TWO

A Living Heritage

IRONICALLY, while the fashionable mania of the late 18th and early 19th Centuries was leading to their apparent discovery in every sort of unlikely or impossible context, the genuine traces of the Druids were there for the finding. Throughout the lands once occupied by the Celts, France and the British Isles, and especially in those places where the influence of invaders was least felt, Brittany, Scotland, Wales, Ireland, Cornwall, the Isle of Man, the Channel Islands, ineradicable prints of Druidism remained. They were to be found in place-names, in folklore, customs, even in language. Their gods were elevated to become Christian saints, ancient kings or the knights of Medieval romance; they survived, too, as the giants and fairies of children's stories and the essential "Celticness" of these has been brilliantly caught by illustrators like Arthur Rackham and Edmond Dulac. In country places, with the participants little knowing what it is they are celebrating, ancient festivals are meticulously kept up. Many, indeed, have been absorbed into the general calendar. There are, of course, innumerable Celtic words in the language (alp, briar, league, vassal, beak, change, for example), but words like "fortnight", the now-obsolete "se'nnight", or the Jersey patois word for "today", *anniet*, which actually means "tonight" are all reminders that the Druids reckoned by nights, not days.

The list of place-names of Celtic derivations is virtually endless and this perhaps is not surprising when one realizes that their influence spread as far as Denmark in the north, Rumania, Germany and Austria in the east, and Italy and Spain in the south. Vienna, Paris and probably Berlin have names drawn from Celtic tribes. Other towns include Arras, Bordeaux, Dover, Milan, Nanterre, Nemours, Venice, and these represent only a random and arbitrary selection from a potential gazetteer of place-names.

Even more significant are the many names which conceal ancient deities. London may come from the name of the god Llud, known elsewhere as Nudd, Nuada or Nodens and often given the surname "the Cloudmaker" or, because he lost a hand in battle and was fitted with a silver prosthesis, as "Nuada of the Silver Hand". He is the apocryphal "King Lud" recalled by the London locations, Ludgate Circus, Ludgate Street and Ludgate Hill.

Toulon comes from the Gaulish deity, Telonia. Lyons and Loudun, changed in form, nevertheless commemorate Lugh the Many Skilled. Bel-Air, Peyrebelle, Aiguebelle and Barenton in France all come from the god-name Belenos, and to this list must be added Beltany Ring in Donegal, which may be less connected with the god himself than with his feast, Beltain. Taransay in the Isle of Harris, can only be named after the Celtic Jupiter, Taranis. As Margaret Killip has been kind enough to point out to me, the same god may be perpetuated in the Isle of Man, not by name, but in the island's symbol of three running legs, probably a form of his attribute, the wheel.

Cornouaille in south west Brittany derives from the Cornovii, literally "People of the Horn", whose migrations also took them to an area which included the modern Shropshire, Cheshire and Staffordshire, as well as to another in the north of Britain, at Caithness. It was once held that the "horn" of their name referred to the promontory of Caithness, but modern opinion, supported by Professor Anne Ross, is that they took it from Cernunnos, the Horned God.

Even family names can recall the old deities. In Ireland and Scotland particularly it would no doubt be possible to pursue many back to these, remembering that all clans liked to trace their lineage to a deity. In Wales, the name of one Other World creature is given in an early myth as "Llwyd" (or, as we would say, "Lloyd"); another, "Pwyll" or "Powell" is probably the original of Pelles, the Fisher-King of the Arthurian legends. One of the most historically distinguished examples must, however, be Bourbon, the name of the royal dynasty which at various times in their history occupied the thrones of France and Naples and at

present occupy that of Spain and who derived their name from the
water-god, Borvo.

We are on still more fertile ground when it comes to river names.
Europe's four principal waterways, the Seine, the Thames, the Rhine
and the Danube all have god-names, while the Marne is a corruption of
Matrona, the mother-goddess, Shannon comes from the deity Sinann,
and Boyne from Boand, "She of the White Cows". In Britain, the Severn
comes from Sabrina, the Wharfe from Verbeia; the Brent in Middlesex
and the Braint in Anglesey from Brigantia, goddess of the immensely
powerful Brigantes, who settled in an area incorporating Cumberland,
Westmorland, Northumberland, Co. Durham, Lancashire and the three
Yorkshire Ridings.

Brigantia, in her turn, may be identical with the Irish goddess, Brigid,
daughter of the Dagda, who survived as the popular St Bridget.
Significantly, the Christian saint, like the pagan goddess, is patron of
cattle and flocks. In Britain her name is associated with scores of holy
wells—the so-called Bridewells or St Bride's Wells. In the Isle of Man,
February 1—St Bridget's Day—is regarded as a crucial date'since the
weather on it is regarded as prophetic foretaste of what will come in the
spring.

In both Scotland and the Hebrides her festival is celebrated and since
she was supposedly the midwife to the Virgin Mary, she was regarded as
the patron of expectant mothers. In many Scottish songs, the saint ming-
les with pagan gods and heroes and even with practices such as human
sacrifice. One actually has an oblique reference to the so-called "triple
death", by fire, drowning and stabbing, with which some sacrificial
victims were dispatched.

Another powerful mother-goddess, Ana or Anu, is perpetuated in the
St Anne's Wells to be found not only all over Britain and Ireland, but
also in Brittany, which province has St Anne as patron saint. If, as some
scholars believe, she is also the deity called Dana or Danu, hers may
have been the womb from which the pre-Celtic gods of Ireland, the
Tuatha De Danann, sprang. Stories of the marvels achieved by the *Tuatha*
are told not only in Ireland, but also in Scotland and Wales.

In Jersey, one of the numerous natural springs in the island was said
to be guarded by two spirits — Arna and Aiuna; in Brittany one of the
most renowned healing wells is that of St Anne d'Auray. Significantly,
the church dedicated to the saint is at Keranna. The Breton prefix
"Ker-" like the Welsh "Caer-" derives from the old Celtic word for
"camp" or "town".

The association between Celtic gods and wells is one found
repeatedly. In the Isle of Man almost every parish has its *chibbyr*. Many
are either curative or wishing wells. One prescribed cure for tooth-ache
still in use is to insert a pin between the teeth then drop it into the water.

Since archaeologists have retrieved pins from wells dating back to Celtic times this is most probably a very ancient custom indeed.

Like the gods to whom they are dedicated, the ceremonies involving wells have also been Christianized. Several of the Breton *Pardons* involve well-blessing — the church of St Anne d'Auray is the destination of one such pilgrimage. Religious rites also take place at another well dedicated to St Anne, that at Buxton in Derbyshire, also supposed to have curative properties.

Brigid and Ana are far from being the only Celtic gods to have achieved canonization. Another is Belenos, venerated in some parts of France as St Bonnet. Ross mentions a "St Llud", beheaded, according to tradition, in Brecknockshire. There is even a "St Taran". Sometimes the process of sanctification goes further and the name changes entirely. So the pagan Lugh becomes "St Michael" and one of the most popular saints of Scotland, though often called, up till the present century, "the god Michael".

But not all have joined the communion of saints. As a horned dweller in a subterranean Other World, the immensely powerful Cernunnos is the generally accepted prototype of the horned Satan of Western Christianity. Perhaps he is not entirely damned, however: on September 13, the people of the Breton town of Carnac, a name which itself contains a *horn*-element, celebrate the *Pardon* of the patron saint of horned animals — St Cornely. Another celebration which must also stem from the worship of Cernunnos — the Festival of the Deermen — takes place in the village of Abbots Bromley in Staffordshire every September 4. (The discrepancy in date between the Breton and the English occasions is probably accounted for by calendrical changes in the two countries.) During the Abbots Bromley festival men wearing headdresses of deer-antlers dance through the streets as an escort to Robin Hood (probably also a Celtic god!). After the ceremony, the spans of antlers are laid up in the church for safekeeping. Carbon dating shows that one of them at least goes back to the year 1065.

Many superstitions, too, can be traced back to Druidic origins. Throwing salt over the shoulder is one. So is the taboo on bringing Maythorn into a house. The custom of kissing under the mistletoe recalls the importance it had for the Druids as well as its obvious fertility connexions.

Ancient beliefs are attached to much of our wildlife. In Man, Jersey and Ireland, the hare and wren were both regarded as prophetic creatures until very recent times. One remembers that before joining battle with the Romans, Boudicca (or Boadicea) loosed a hare from beneath her cloak that it might predict the outcome of the struggle. In the Isle of

Man, they are regarded as transformed witches. In both Man and Jersey, the wren, believed to presage disaster, was the quarry of an annual hunt on St Stephen's Day, December 26. In Jersey this was finally banned in 1930; in the Isle of Man, while it is still practised, the live creature has given place to a symbolic bunch of feathers carried from house to house.

Stranger customs still are associated with death and the dead. The classical sources recall that the Celtic conviction of survival after death was such that they were prepared to accept debts "payable in the next life". In another reference there is a description of the custom of burning letters to the deceased on his funeral pyre, in the belief that he would thus be able to read them in the Other World. Survivals of such notions are still to be found. In Man, a debt was often sworn over a grave and this form of oath had legal standing until the 17th Century. Sabine Baring-Gould, in a work on Brittany written in the early years of the century, lists numerous customs in which the dead are treated as being accessible to the living.

The abortive plot of Guy Fawkes and his co-conspirators is surely a curious event to commemorate so faithfully. If an excuse for letting off fireworks is needed, a moment's thought could provide a dozen or so infinitely more important events in British history. One might be the defeat of the Spanish Armada, instrumental in destroying Catholic domination. But is it no more than coincidence that November 5 falls so close to the Celtic festival of the dead, Samain, on November 1, an occasion marked by burning human offerings? The sinister ambiguity of the guy is emphasized in Jersey folklore. There a custom similar to the Yule logs of Northern Europe was kept up: a large baulk of wood was gathered, dressed up in clothes then burnt on the last night of the year, under the name of *le vieux bout de l'an*, the end of the old year, a practice still being condemned as late as Puritan times. After the introduction of Guy Fawkes celebrations, the term *boudelau*, a corruption of *bout de l'an* was applied by country people to a guy and was still in use in my own boyhood.

Besides its likely connexion with the Gun Powder Plot, Samain must also be perpetuated in the semi-magical festival of Hallowe'en. At Kirkwall in the Orkneys, indeed, Guy Fawkes and Hallowe'en actually have become confused and throughout the islands the traces of sacrifice can be found in local celebrations. The day is observed as a day-long fast, but at its end each family kills a castrated ram or wether and eats it at a Hallowmas banquet.

In Scotland, Hallowe'en is often celebrated on November 11, thus keeping to the old calendar[1]. The occasion was marked by enormous

---

[1] Is it also coincidence that another Festival of the Dead — Remembrance Sunday — is also kept up on 11 November or as close as possible to it?

bonfires, the chosen site for these being the tops of tumuli or prehistoric burial mounds, in itself a perpetuation of a pagan Celtic custom. Samain was the time that these mounds, the *sidh*s in Ireland, opened and their dwellers tried to lure the living to join them. In the legend of Condle the Red, the young hero, son of Conn of the Hundred Battles, is tempted by a lovely creature only he can see to a land, inhabited only by women, which lies within the *sidh*. For all the efforts of the king's Druid to prevent him, he leaves father and family and sails away in a glass fairy-boat, never to be heard of more.

A Manx story tells how two farm workers, on their way to a smithy to have a plough-bar straightened on All Hallows' Eve, were lured by fair women into a house. One drank from the proferred cup and joined the wild dance. The other refused and shortly afterwards departed, alone. The other was not seen until a year later, when his friend, passing the same way again, saw the house and its seductive occupants with his rash companion still dancing in their midst.

But it was not only from the *sidh*s that peril threatened. This was the time when the other entrance to the world of the dead could draw the living to it. Cities, like the Breton Ys, rose up from beneath the waves, and stories of such submerged cities are to be found all round the coasts of the British Isles and the other Celtic lands. A Breton story, still told, relates how the lovely Soutbinen gave rowdy parties at her house by the sea and how a tunnel leading from it to the depths beneath the waters was found.

Almost all our own festivals and Bank Holidays mark the great pagan occasions and were, indeed, introduced to supplant the veneration of the pagan deities. Christmas, as we know, was given its particular position in the calendar to divert attention from the old mid-winter celebration and has done so with such notable success that only vestiges of paganism now remain. This has also been the case with Easter, though in both cases we have to remember the antique myth which lies at the root even of the Christian one, that of the young god, miraculously born, who sacrifices himself and goes down into the Underworld there to procure some benefit for humanity. Often, as with the Egyptian Isis and Horus, he is the one associated with the sun. This imparts a special significance to the spring festival when, the gray god of winter defeated, the disk of the sun returns to the heavens and all living things can partake of its warmth and life-giving radiance.

The Celtic god of the sun was Belenos the Brilliant, whose feast was at the beginning of May marking the time when the cattle left their winter quarters for the open, summer pastures. The festival of Beltaine (literally "The Fires of Beli") was marked like Samain, with human sacrifice and by the lighting of enormous bonfires between which the cattle were driven to exorcize the evil spirits which might have taken up lodging in their midst through the winter. Survivals of this were to be found until very recent times in both the Highlands and Ireland. In the Isle of Man, too, hillside gorse and hedgerows were set ablaze "to burn out the witches", while skin drums were beaten and horns blown throughout the day — a noisy ritual with a peculiarly Druidic ring about it. As further protection against witches crosses made from twigs of the mountain-ash — a tree highly venerated by the Druids — were twisted into crosses to be hidden in the tails of cattle, and houses and cattle-sheds were decorated with spring flowers such as primroses.

In the Shetlands, bonfires were lit during the Beltain Fair. Round these, boys and men danced, making it a point of honour to jump through the flames. Another Beltain custom involved the passing of a burning peat turf from hand to hand while a rhyme was repeated. Whoever had the turf when it went out was required to pay a special forfeit. Going down on all fours, like an animal, his back was piled up with rubbish. But it was, otherwise, a period when people kept to their home for three days, acknowledging the fact that this was the festival of the god governing the sun by looking skyward to greet it with the words "Good morning and show your eye".

Here, too, as well as in the Orkneys, this was the occasion when the sick visited wells which were circled sun-wise before drinking from them, another tribute to Belenos, who was also a god of healing, like the Graeco-Roman Apollo. The same custom of well-visiting was also to be found in Man, where one of the wells is actually called "Chibbyr Beltain".

These cultural heirlooms were by no means the sole possession of the strictly Celtic peoples. The Maypoles erected on English village greens must surely also have descended from the sun-god's festival — the phallic qualities of the pole and its fertility associations are obvious enough. And is it not reasonable to suppose that the "May Queen", traditionally the prettiest and most virtuous girl in the village, was chosen to be mate for the deity and hence was the sacrificial victim?

The Helston Floral Dance and the Padstow Hobby-Horse, festivals still celebrated in Cornwall, no doubt have a similar history and it is significant that, as T. C. Lethbridge has pointed out, Helston derives from Hele Stone, "stone of the sun".

The church declared midsummer's day to be the Festival of St John the Baptist and the patronage of so important a saint — the cousin or, some say, brother of Christ — indicates that he was intended to displace some equally important deity. In Man it was the custom to wear a sprig of St John's Wort to mark the day, but in the early 19th Century members of the island's parliament, the House of Keys, adopted mug-wort, *Artemisia vulgaris*, a local plant. As Stenning points out, this bears the

name of Artemis or Diana, a prominent fertility goddess whose festival
was actually celebrated on St John's Day. In Graeco-Roman mythology
Artemis is the sister of Apollo whose Celtic equivalent is Belenos. There
is a strong possibility of a link between Apollo and Belenos, so that a
connexion between Artemis/Diana and one of the Celtic feminine deities
is also likely.

In Jersey it was customary for fishermen to row round a rock called
"Le Cheval Guillaume" in St John's Bay on this day. There are also
stories of bonfires' being lit and of "Bacchanalian dancing" round them
in a tradition similar to one found in the Isle of Man, where it was said
the revels were "too shocking to be told". In both cases the terminology
employed by observers is immediately reminiscent of the descriptions of
the later witchcraft practices.

August Bank Holiday, the old Lammastide, coincides with Lugnasad,
the festival of Lugh. Lugh the Many Skilled, often equated with Mercury
and like him patron of the arts, crafts and of traders, reputedly dedicated
it to his foster-mother, Tailtiu, but the triple Macha, inter alia an Earth
Goddess, was probably also invoked on this day. In Man, which has a
special connexion with Lugh as he was supposed to have spent his
childhood with his foster-parents there, the festival is interpreted as a
contest between the young god and Crom Dubh (? Black Claw) in
which, by his victory, corn is given to the people. Until recent times the
first Sunday in August was marked in the island by crowds ascending to
the mountain tops and one observer comments that the inhabitants of
Kirk Lonan behaved "very rudely and indecently".

At Kirkwall, in the Orkneys, the Lammas Fair was the most important event in the local calendar and included a custom so at variance
with the island's strict Presbyterian code that one must suspect a pre-
Christian origin. For the period of the fair, young men and girls picked
"Lammas" brothers or sisters. Rows of sheaves, called a "lang bed",
were laid out on barn floors and, after the girls had spent an evening
carding wool, they would be joined on these by the young men.

The "Harvest Festivals" and "Harvest Homes" which take place
throughout the British Isles must be similar relics and there is the long
ancestry of "corn dollies", figurines made out of the last sheaf to be
garnered and by tradition buried in the field to ensure a plentiful harvest
the following year.

One is far from having exhausted the links with the present and the
Celtic pagan past: others will be mentioned in the pages of this book, all
attesting to the strength of belief in a supernatural world, a Celtic
characteristic which, we know, so impressed outside observers.

Superstition is still a quality associated with Celts and, as evidence of this, there is the prevalent and strongly-held belief in second-sight and in people gifted with it found especially in Scotland and Ireland. In all the Celtic lands "witches", male or female, have played and to a greater or lesser extent still play a central role in life. Their talents include water-divining, wart-charming, herb-medicine, fortune-telling and, often, the casting of spells or counter-spells. Similar skills were almost certainly possessed by the Druids.

It would be rash, indeed absurd, to suggest that these are their lineal successors. But there is good reason for believing that at least some part of Druidic wisdom has survived — a point we shall have reason to return to. There are at any rate two interesting linguistic pointers. The Manx Celtic word for wizard is *Fer-Druaight* which is surely cognate with "Druid", while the word "guee" meaning both to pray and to curse, bears a close resemblance to the exclusively Druidic form of spell-casting, the *geas*, a type of taboo whose violation meant certain death and which is still taken seriously in the Scottish Highlands.

CHAPTER THREE

Celtic Civilization

WHO were the bearers of a system of beliefs so extraordinarily tenacious?

The Spanish Franciscans who went to the newly conquered lands of Central and South America in the 15th Century expected to find the natives, members of a culture which practised human sacrifice on what can only be called a lavish scale, grim and blood-thirsty barbarians. Instead they found a people who were intelligent, good-humoured, courteous, and hospitable. At a distance, the Celts, too, would have been seen as the pathetic, half-brute creatures of heathen lands.

The similarities between the civilizations discovered and wantonly destroyed by the Conquistadores and that earlier one ravaged by the Romans are numerous and remarkable, and we know that, despite Tacitus' propagandist zeal in making the Celts and especially the Druids appear dark, sinister and sanguinary, their actual character was quite different. Cicero's encounter with Diviciacus makes this much plain.

Nor, by contrast were they the fey inhabitants of that ethereal half-world bequeathed to us by the romantics from Tennyson to Yeats. The real truth about the Celtic peoples is that they were a race of great originality, of artistic creativity and aggressive dynamism. They were, for example, among Europe's first iron users. Their artistic skill has led to their being called the most original creators north of the Alps. Their questing expansionism established them as masters of a vast province not only in Europe, but which stretched down into Asia Minor. The Greeks categorized them, with the Scythians and the Iberians, as one of the three great barbarian nations and with the rest of the ancient world viewed them with that terror later to be inspired by "the Mongol hordes".

In 390 BC the Romans, rather imprudently allowing themselves to become embroiled in a war between the Celts and Etruscans, found themselves the objective of a punitive expedition. Their attackers, advancing down the Italic peninsula, reached and sacked the Eternal City, putting to the sword those few patricians too proud to flee. Only a small enclave of refugees succeeded in holding out on a besieged Capitoline Hill, an occasion memorable for the famous incident in which the cries of the sacred geese gave warning of impending assault, saving the Temple of Jupiter from desecration. Nonetheless, as the price of their withdrawal, the besiegers demanded and received an extortionate ransom, which led to another famous incident: when the Romans complained that false scales were being used to weigh out the bullion, the Celtic commander threw his sword into the scale pan, thus increasing the weight, with the cry, *Vae victis*! — Woe to the vanquished!

A hundred and ten years after their attack on Rome another Celtic expeditionary force attempted to march on Delphi, where the Oracle itself was saved only by a sudden and unexpected onset of winter snow, thus vindicating its own prediction that it would be "saved by the white virgins". With this reversal in their fortunes, the Celtic commanders were forced to kill off their own wounded to secure a rapid escape.

In 225 BC, Rome was once more threatened and it took three armies to stay the onslaught at the Battle of Telamon, though not before one had been annihilated.

Where had it come from, this terrifying race which could defy even Rome?

About the middle of the Second Millennium BC, the tribes of pastoral and hunting nomads — the so-called Indo-Europeans — who inhabited an area round the Caspian Sea in south Russia began to spread eastwards and westwards. The westward thrust took them across the European Plain, down through the Balkans, into Greece and Italy and over the Mediterranean into Asia Minor, as well as northward into Scandinavia whose climate was at that time so temperate that wine-grapes were grown in what is now Norway. In all the places of their settlement, in admixture with the far more numerous existing populations, the Indo-Europeans provided the racial and linguistic matrix for most of the nations of Europe — including the Greeks and Romans.

But it was not until the 10th Century BC that a people recognizably Celtic began to emerge in an area roughly centring on what is now Bohemia. In a period between the 8th and 6th Centuries BC, they began fresh migrations which carried them into northern Italy, Spain, parts of Scandinavia, as well as France and Belgium, and later into the British Isles.

Their various migrations and their sojourn in their Bohemian homeland, "the cockpit of Europe", had brought them into contact with many other cultures, of which the Scythian particularly exerted a lasting influence upon them. The Greek, Polybius, who wrote a contemporary account of the Battle of Telamon, describes in detail the enemy tactics: the terrifying noise of their trumpets and war-chants and their use of two-wheeled and four-wheeled chariots, the manufacture and employment of which they must have learnt from the Scythians, one of the first races to domesticate the horse.

Also Scythian were their moustaches so thick it was said they served as strainers when they drank, and their odd custom of treating their hair with lime wash, which not only bleached it, but made it stand back from their heads like the mane of a horse — a fashion illustrated on some Celtic coinage.

Even in their manner of dress they imitated the Scythians: the breeches, obviously intended for horse-riding, but quite alien to the Mediterranean world of Polybius; their linen tunics reaching to the knees, and the cloaks they wore over them. These last, of purple, crimson or green dyed woven wool, or of tartan design, can only have been the predecessors of the plaids worn in Scotland and Ireland and the Welsh shawls.

With costume went another aspect of their appearance which enhanced an appearance already dauntingly weird to foreign eyes. They were, we are told, exceptionally tall. In part, this may have been by comparison with the slighter southern build, but one can scarcely ignore the evidence of their size from elsewhere. Giants figure repeatedly as the villains of Norse myth. Thor was said so to have hated them he killed them with his hammer on sight. The Celtic incursions into Scandinavia must have brought them into collision with existing inhabitants of the region. The stories of ensuing battles against tall enemies, passed orally from generation to generation, would gradually have become assimilated into legendary struggles between Norse heroes and giants.

A further association between Celts and giants is to be found in Diodorus of Sicily, who flourished about 40 BC. He attributed the foundation of Celtiberia, the Celtic region of Spain, now Galicia, to the mating of Hercules — whom Pythagoras characterizes as a giant — with a local princess.

As the physical appearance of the Celts so impressed observers by its strangeness, their environment, too, must have seemed quite unlike the bustling, teeming cities of Mediterranean and Aegean seaboards. In Gaul, where cities were found at all, they were usually sited near Greek or Roman settlements, and demonstrative, therefore, of a desire to emulate.

Overall the Celtic landscape was one largely of forest, dotted with isolated farmsteads, often enclosed behind high walls of stone or wood, like miniature fortresses, much like the farms in the Channel Islands today. The largest centres of population in Gaul, Britain or Ireland would have seemed scarcely more than villages to outsiders. In *The Conquest of Gaul*, Caesar describes the groups of hilltop dwellings, surrounded by their defensive palisades, which he calls *oppida*, and he mentions the difficulties facing an attacker trying to find means of scaling the formidable structure of steep walls and ramparts. Remains found by archaeologists, such as those at Mont Beurray in Burgundy, bear him out.

Behind this shield, the dry-stone houses, often circular in shape and with deep-pitched thatched roofs, stood round an open, central area, as has been found at Heuneberg in Austria. In the story of the naming of Cu Chulainn in the Irish *Cattle Raid of Cooley*, King Conchobhar of Ulster first encounters the boy demonstrating his prowess at a game like football "on the green" and one can suppose that, like those of English villages, such areas functioned not only as a playground, but also as places of assembly.

In the actual buildings, though mortar was not employed, for those points such as door lintels where movement had to be obviated, joints were constructed by a system of wooden pegs fitting into matching holes in the abutting stones. The Etruscans used a similar technique and Kendrick believes it to have been copied from them.

The internal decoration would obviously vary with the wealth of the owner. But a description, also in *The Cattle Raid*, tells us that Conchobhar's house had 150 inner rooms, panelled in red yew. The king's own room in the centre, was guarded "by screens of copper, with bars of silver and gold birds on the screens, and precious jewels in the birds' heads for eyes". The passage also describes some of the other rooms of Conchobhar's palace, including the armoury which "twinkled with the gold of sword-hilts and the gold and silver glimmering on the necks and coils of grey javelins, on shield-plates and shield-rims, and in the sets of goblets, cups and drinking horns". The length of the description and its detail is indicative of the interest in home decoration shown by the Celts.

Wherever they settled, the Celts brought the benefit of improved agriculture and animal husbandry. Thanks to their use of the iron plough they were able vastly to increase the productivity of the land, while as cattle- and particularly as horse-breeders, they pioneered many advances. A measure of this is the fact that almost all the words in Latin connected with horses and horse-management are Celtic loan-words.

For the cultivation of cereals, the plains of Gaul were obviously the more ideally suited, so that although some were grown in Britain and Ireland, these islands were principally given over to livestock rearing.

A thriving trade in farm-products was complemented by other exports, such as of metals, in the forms both of ingot and finished products, and of salt, for which there was a high demand in the ancient world. This prosperity enabled them to import a wide range of goods, among them many luxuries, especially wines from the Mediterranean vineyards. For these they had developed so inordinate a fondness that it inspired derisive comment by the classical writers, besides yielding unsurpassed opportunities to unscrupulous vintners, by whom it was said that the Celts would offer a slave for a jug of wine, a servant for a single swallow.

It also allowed them to indulge their taste for personal adornment by importing precious metals and gems. Their woollen cloaks were secured by a pin or brooch, often intricately wrought from gold or silver (though for the poor, we are told, a thorn had to suffice). Both sexes, who in general dressed similarly, wore rings, armlets and bracelets and had ornate buckles to their belts often, like Conchobhar's birds, studded with jewels. Articles of this kind have been found among grave goods, together with wrought and inlaid weapons. Indeed, a preoccupation with ornamentation and appearance was so prominent a feature of the Celtic character that it finds reflection in legend. In one of the early Irish stories, for example, Loegh, charioteer to the hero, Cu Chulainn, details the dress of another, approaching charioteer: " ... A crimson cloak round him with a golden brooch in it, and a hooded tunic with red embroidery on him. A convex shield with a rim of ornamented white bronze on it ...". In another story, that of Etain, the appearance of one of the characters is described in even more detail. We are told that an approaching horseman has a "long, flowing green cloak behind him, a shirt embroidered with red gold and a huge brooch of gold at his throat reaching to either shoulder".

In the production of these and other items they were by no means dependent on foreign craftsmen. They had themselves developed techniques for enamelling and their own artists possessed a brilliant creative originality. It was the discovery made at La Tène, a shallow area in Lake Neuchâtel in Switzerland, in 1858, which first made archaeologists aware that the Celts were by no means the artless barbarians as had once been supposed. The hoard included swords, spears, fibulae and tools, all testifying to enormous skill and confidence in the handling of metals. Other, though less dramatic, discoveries have come from river beds, lake bottoms, wells and shafts all over the Celtic world and there is no doubt much more to be found. Work similar to that discovered at La Tène was probably still being produced in Ireland as late as the 3rd and 4th Centuries AD. The designs, those patterns of intertwining tendrils which have come to be regarded as typical, sprang directly from the forms of nature, as observers of which the Celts have never been surpassed. Even their most modest work reflects not just the contours but the very essence of the living world, its shapes, motion and rhythms.

The talent of their craftsmen was matched in other spheres. Though literate, the Celts used writing principally for account keeping or for inscriptions such as on coins. The reason for this was that their concepts of history, law and practical knowledge were all believed to be of sacred origin. Their exposure to written form might accordingly lead to devaluation and sacrilege.

The practical effect was, however, that there was no written literature, though there was a brilliant and vigorous oral one. The trustees of this were the bards, who stood close to the nobility in the social hierarchy, "a nobility of art", in Markale's words, enjoying special privileges. The epics and eulogies which formed the bardic repertory were certainly designed to be sung to their own accompaniment and the harp has become an instrument closely associated with the Celts.

There are, as we shall see, good reasons for associating the Druids with this thriving creative life.

The manifest artistry of the Celts drew little response from their classical observers. Like Victorian travellers in Africa who saw in, say, a Benin bronze just the distortions of a pathetic primitivism, they could only contrast the fighting, feasting and fornicating barbarians of the Celtic lands with the home life of their own dear Royal Family where, admittedly, guests at banquets did not reject the charms of the ladies — for all that they are shown to us as Amazons — in favour of open sexual frolics on animal skins with their boy friends.

Blinded by xenophobia, the classical writers failed also to perceive that though different from their own world, Celtic society still displayed a cultural homogeneity which proclaimed it to be an organic entity, governed by customs, institutions and laws no less comprehensive than theirs.

Good manners, courtesy and particularly hospitality marked Celtic social life and extended to strangers whose primary needs of food, drink and shelter had to be satisfied before any inquiry was made about their presence or intentions, and, like so much else, this has survived down to the present day in the renowned hospitality of the Celtic peoples. Even those great feasts to which they were so addicted were far from being orgies of animal gluttony. Guests sat on hay or skins before a low table, their position being governed by an etiquette of precedence in which the visitor was always accorded a high place. Food served included roast or boiled meats, beef, mutton and especially pork, the "champion's portion" being allegedly a whole roast boar. The meat was accompanied by bread and there would be locally brewed beer and mead, as well as imported wine.

On such occasions they undoubtedly drank to excess, yet this over-indulgence must have been the exception for, because no doubt in a warrior society a fat man made a poor fighter, obesity was a punishable offence.

Among the peculiarly Celtic customs mentioned by Caesar and confirmed elsewhere is that of fosterage which continued down into Christian times. (King Arthur was fostered and we are told that Kai was his foster-brother.) Under the system as practised, the responsibility for the upbringing and education of a child was taken over by others and he did not return to the bosom of his own family until puberty.

Outside the purely traditional and customary, there was a strict legal code, largely as we shall see administered by the Druids, and transmitted orally. This, too, has survived in some measure. A class of itinerant jurists, the *brehons*, existed in Ireland down to Elizabethan times when, with an associated body of poets, it was among the first victims of the terror imposed by the Queen's Commissioners. In the Isle of Man, the unwritten "Breast Law", derived from the decisions of successive Deemsters, or local justices, is regarded as no less binding than the written law, which did not come into existence until 1423. In the Channel Islands those numerous precedents, so colourfully alluded to as "lost in the mists of time", must have been unwritten.

Among other things, Celtic law guaranteed the place of women, who could own property, even if married; could choose their own husbands; could divorce and were entitled to substantial damages at law if deserted or molested. Women played an important part in political life; could take their place in the battle line and could even ascend to the chieftaincy. In general, the role they play in Celtic life reminds one of that found in some Asiatic societies, particularly in Thailand and Tibet, where men and women share even manual labour and these surprising coincidences are ones which we shall find frequently recurring.

The survival of matrilineal descent in both Wales and Ireland whereby a man is described not as his father's, but as his mother's son, so that, for example, King Conchobhar is called 'Conchobhar mac Nessa', after his mother, no doubt arose originally from the ignorance of the male role in conception and from the loose nature of sexual ties.

Though Caesar was certainly exaggerating in his description of the depressed condition of the plebians, Celtic society was a slave-owning and aristocratic one, even though its leaders may have been men of shrewdness, capability and, above all, of taste.

The social base was the clan and the tribe, itself a grouping of several clans under a chieftain or king called a *rig*. The Celtic clan, called a *fine*, was rather different from those of Scotland and Ireland as they were later known. The foundation of the clan was a common ancestor, hence the prefix "Mac-", "son of ...". This made possible a potentially infinite extension as sons married, begat and their sons did similarly. The *fine*, instead, was restricted to four generations, from father to great-grandson. Thereafter, there was a splitting with a compulsory sharing of commonly held property.

The head of the *fine* had his tribal counterpart — the *rig*. To an extent hereditary, in that he was always chosen from a single royal *fine*, there was no automatic succession from father to son. When a chieftain died, the choice of successor was a matter for deliberation by a tribal assembly at which all the *fines* were represented, but in which — as we shall see — the Druids played the crucial role.

The *rig* or chieftain's domain was not defined territorially, but by its people, the *tuatha*, a Celtic word from which the name of the god, Toutatis or Teutatis (?God of the People) as well as the word Teutonic may be derived. The consolidation of the *fines* which the *tuatha* represented was, no doubt, the first tentative step in the evolution towards nationhood, but as has happened elsewhere, the jealous rivalries which developed between tribes were such as successfully to prevent political unification. The Celts of Ireland, Britain and Gaul were, therefore, never anything but a loose confederation of tribes gathered within a given land area.

Sometimes, however, a tribe might itself split and part of it migrate, so that tribal names occur twice, often at places distant from one another on maps of the Celtic world. This would perhaps indicate that the division was the result of internal quarrels, possibly over succession, but it could also have occurred because a particular region was becoming over-populated in relation to its land-resources. The Atrebates, who had settled in an area of France round Arras which takes its name from them, are to be found, as well, in a region roughly corresponding to Berkshire and parts of Wiltshire in Britain. The Parisii, who gave their name to Paris, also established themselves in the East Riding of Yorkshire.

Choice of chieftain was by no means the only matter referred to the tribal assemblies all of which, as we know from Strabo, were governed by strict rules of discussion. Some would have taken place on the central green in the townships, but the more important ones, such as those held during the religious festivals, took place near the royal burial place. In most tribal societies, the link between its living and its dead is of supreme importance and in this the Celtic was no exception. Although it is of Norse origin, one is reminded of the annual meeting at Tynwald on the Isle of Man, held under the presidency of the Lieutenant-Governor as representative of the British monarch. It is significant that Tynwald Hill is itself actually a tumulus or burial mound.

Given the form of their society, it is not difficult to understand the need for such communal decision-making. Despite its essentially hierarchic nature, Celtic society did not possess the pyramidal structure of inter-connected allegiances to be found in feudal ones, where each class stood in utter dependence upon the next one above it. Here the social bond was the custom of *celsine* or cliency. The essence of this was that a *fine* or even an individual placed himself under another's protection, rendering in return agreed payments in kind, as well as armed service if it were required of him. No sacrifice of rights or liberties was involved and the *cele* or client could freely withdraw from the arrangement.

In origin *celsine* must have dated back to the times when land-winning expeditions were being mounted, but no doubt they would also have been entered into after natural disasters such as the failure of the harvest had afflicted a particular tribe or when, for example, inter-clan or inter-tribal feuds broke out. The last were probably common, for lacking the public administration of law through a permanent system of courts, the settlement of many grievances would have been an individual or clan matter, and we know that feuding persisted late into Scottish history. Faced with such external threats, the weaker party might well feel it prudent to place itself under the wing of a more powerful one.

In actual practice, *celsine* would probably have become a mutually dependent arrangement, for while the *cele* needed the protection of the stronger unit, his patron would measure his power as well his prestige and actual wealth by the number of his *cele*s. It is also significant that land tenure was by *fine* and not by individual so that each family with its holding represented a lesser domain within the larger one of the *tuatha*. (It is of course the reason why clan areas are to be found in Scotland and Ireland.) Because of this, the extent of tribal territory would also be decided by the number of *cele*s constituting it, each of whom was basically an independent unit[1].

[1] In this connexion, the Channel Islands afford an interesting parallel. The "parishes" into which Jersey and Guernsey are divided must once have corresponded with clan areas. In earlier times,

As a grouping of at least theoretically free entities, mutual agreement in all decisions would obviously be essential and there are good reasons for thinking that this was far from being a pure formality. Everyone in Celtic society was not only conscious of, but exercised his rights and freedoms as Strabo among others tells us. Indeed, it was as a result of this that the Celtic regions proved so resistant to feudalism and in many instances avoided it altogether.

Markale suggests that the tribal assembly was the supreme authority in Celtic society, implying that when they took place the chieftain's role was little more than that of chairman, which accords with our knowledge, for it is obvious that he did not enjoy the unquestioned dominance to be found elsewhere. This, of course, is most noteworthy in religious matters, for where, in other cultures, the chieftain or king was principal mediator with the gods on his people's behalf, in the case of the Celts this was the prerogative and perhaps the monopoly of the Druids.

In war, the chief delegated his powers of leadership to an elected war-chief. The leaders of expeditions against Rome and Delphi are nowhere mentioned as chieftains. In the cycle of Irish stories, the warrior-hero is Cu Chulainn, not the king, Conchobhar. In the Arthurian legends the king is repeatedly found, less as commander in battle (though in the first historical references Arthur is mentioned as a *dux bellorum* or war-leader), than as rewarder of heroes, and arbitrator in disputes.

There was good enough reason for this. In the case of both the march on Rome and that on Delphi a century later we have the same name given as that of the Celtic commander — Brennos or Brennius. The explanation once offered was that two men of the same name were involved, the later perhaps the descendant of the earlier. The truth is that Brennos is the name of a Celtic god, otherwise Brân or Brân Vendigeit — Brân the Blessed. What we have then is a military expedition under, as it were, divine patronage, in other words "a holy war". This raised it above the purely tribal conflicts, attracting to its banner warriors from the entire Celtic world. References to continental expeditions occur in both Irish myth and in the much later Geoffrey of Monmouth, who has two brothers Belinus (obviously Belenos) and Brennius attacking Rome. If command had been entrusted to a tribal chief there would have been the risk of intertribal rivalries breaking out during the actual campaign, as they sometimes did, anyway.

There was, however, a second link uniting *fine* and *tuatha*. This was the

---

major decisions were taken through *l'ouie de la paroisse* — a parish meeting. This continues today through what are called the Parish Assemblies, which all rate-paying householders are entitled to attend.

religious one. Whether *celsine* contracts actually incorporated a clause whereby the client invoked the gods of his patron we have no way of knowing. We can conclude, all the same, that even if the clan deities were not abandoned when it became a client the tribal ones, in origin probably those of the "royal" *fine*, were also venerated. We have evidence, for example, of the separate communities within a tribe being expected to provide victims for sacrifice. As we saw many tribes took their names from gods like the powerful Brigantes, who spread over much of Northern England.

By general consensus among the classical writers, the Celts were an extremely superstitious people. Since superstition was not a thing either Greek or Roman was totally free from, Celtic conduct, in their ordinary affairs, must have been such as to display a more than normal concern with the supernatural. Their divination and human sacrifice we know shocked and fascinated outside observers, but there were other surprising Celtic practices. Polybius, at the Battle of Telamon, was struck by the appearance in combat of naked *gestatae* or spear-throwers, and a practice so contrary to the instinct of self-preservation seems likely to have had a religious basis. Another custom was the wearing of the torc or neck-band of twisted metal, apparently common to all sectors of Celtic society, with only the costliness of the metal involved distinguishing the classes. Since torcs are presented on even the most rudimentary images of their gods, this too must have had a religious significance.

Strabo refers to Gaulish warriors returning from the fray, carrying hung from their saddles, the severed heads of those who had fallen at their hands. These grisly trophies were also to be found decorating the exteriors of houses and the same author mentions instances of heads being embalmed in cedar oil and shown off to guests.

For this custom there is a wealth of supportive archaeological and other evidence. Niches cut into door lintels must have been for the display of heads, and skulls with nails driven through them have been found. In surviving myth the decapitation of enemies is a recurrent motif, down to the Arthurian legends and beyond. In the 14th Century story of *Gawain and the Green Knight*, the hero is challenged to decapitate the Green Knight. If he succeeds, as Gawain does, he must meet his rival who obviously survives the blow in single combat a year later. The knight is plainly, if not a god, at least an Other World being and the entire story bears marked similarities with earlier pagan ones.

If religion and the worship of particular gods assisted the process of cementing the *fine* to the *tuatha*, it can also be shown that they actually impeded the progression from a tribal to a national identity. Nationhood would have involved the acceptance of a state pantheon. This would have meant that either new gods would have to come into being or that existing ones would have to be elevated to this new, greater role. It would also have meant the degradation of other deities.

The unwillingness of the Celtic tribes to cooperate in such a process is indicated by the very large number of deities which iconographers have identified, something approaching 400, of which the majority must have been local or exclusively tribal. But there were, besides, those gods associated with features of the landscape, especially rivers or other water sources. The demotion of these, or their supersession by others would, of course, have been to risk the anger of divine forces which as territorial deities were unhealthily close at hand for the tribes involved.

CHAPTER FOUR

Witnesses and Their Testimony

CELTIC religion is, as Caesar declares, the province of the Druids. Diogenes Laertius (AD 200-250) makes clear that Druidism was regarded as an ancient institution in the times of Aristotle, the 4th Century BC. This gains at least partial support from other information: one of the earliest references to the Celts occurs about the 5th Century BC. It records a meeting between Alexander the Great and a Celt, possibly a Druid. Certainly the brief interview contained one phrase with an unmistakably Druidic ring: Alexander asked his visitor what it was his people most feared? He was told, nothing "so long as the sky does not fall or the sea burst its limits".

Those words re-echo down the centuries. They occur twice in *The Cattle Raid of Cooley*. Once when things are going amiss, Sualdam seeks to put new heart into the Ulstermen: "Are the heavens rent?" he asks; "Is the sea bursting its bounds? Is the end of the world upon us?" Later, the warriors of Conchobhar assure him: "We will hold out until the earth gives under us, or until the heavens fall on us and make us give way."

In the 5th Century AD we find it being employed in only slightly altered form by the bards Taliesin and Myrddin. Thus, Myrddin: "Since the Battle of Arderydd, nothing can touch me — even if the sky falls and the sea overflows."

Yet, for all the antiquity of Druidism, for all the contacts between the Celts and other nations, for all the fascination they evoked, nowhere do we find a systematic account of their religion, and this stands in sharp contrast with the body of often explicit detail about Celtic life in general. The Druids, who took such pains to invest themselves and their teachings with mystery and secrecy, may perhaps have succeeded better than they knew: if ever they stood guardians of the founts of an Ancient Wisdom they certainly ensured its treasures were not passed on.

Obviously their reluctance to commit their teachings to writing is in a large measure to blame for this, forcing us to rely on enigmatic hints and on fragmentary and second-hand information as it is offered to us by the small band of alien observers of Celtic life.

Of these, two have contributed most to delineating the popular conception of the Druids.

In countless illustrations adorning books down the ages, their full-bearded figures are portrayed standing among the oaks of some forest glade, knife poised over human victim; or hacking mistletoe from amid the tree's branches with their golden sickles. These images and the white robes which have become the universal insignia of those "Druidic" brotherhoods, descending from the group round Iolo Morganwg's pebble *gorsedd*, owe their sanction to a single reference in the Elder Pliny's *Natural History*. This and a famous passage on sacrifice in Caesar's *The Conquest of Gaul* are the two best known accounts of Druidism in action.

Pliny we know to have been a keen observer — he was killed in AD 79 when he approached too close to Vesuvius to study its eruption. His *Natural History* was dedicated to Titus, later emperor, and dated two years before its author's death. Since it is made up of some thirty-seven books, production must have been spread over many years, but in AD 37, with Gaul firmly under Roman control, Tiberius issued his edict prohibiting the practices of Druidism. This would have made first-hand study of it extremely difficult so that his information probably came from other, earlier sources.

The book is actually a discursive account of the state of what we should now call "scientific knowledge" and, for the modern reader, it is its very digressions which are among its greatest attractions. They take the form of illustrative anecdotes, hence the description of mistletoe in what is actually a general account of the medicinal properties of herbs. It was, he tells us, held in the highest awe by the Gaulish Druids especially when found growing on an oak-tree, a comparatively rare occurrence. What gave it this special character was that oak itself was so venerated that groves of it were chosen as the centres of Druidic worship. In consequence, anything which grew on it was regarded as divinely sent, as further proof that the tree was "chosen by the god himself", though he neglects to state which god.

Besides the famous description of the mistletoe gathering, Pliny also tells us of two other herbs held in high esteem by the Druids, as well as how they were ritually gathered, and of a magic egg called *anguinem* — supposedly made from the secretion of snakes — said to "ensure success in lawsuits and a favourable reception with princes".

What he gives us, then, are some fascinating snapshots of specific activities, but it would take a good many such before we should have anything like "A Day in the Life of a Druid". Indeed, as we shall see, Pliny may actually have been responsible for distorting our image, because his information about what are special events has been interpreted by others as having general validity.

Set beside Pliny's close-ups, Caesar's viewpoint is panoramic and that he was contemporary with the matter he was describing gives it added attraction. As commander-in-chief of the Roman forces he travelled in Gaul and hence had unrivalled opportunities for obtaining information. Thus he is able to tell us about the structure of Celtic society; of the central role of the Druids in religious life; of the variety of their functions; of the importance of sacrifice; of their recruitment, training and organization; and he provides us with a list of the most important gods worshipped by the Gauls, though giving them under their Roman equivalents.

He has to be treated with scepticism, none the less. Firstly, he was pre-eminently an interested party. He was in Gaul as an invader and one of his intentions in writing *The Conquest* must certainly have been to justify himself in the eyes of the senate and people of Rome. Hence, he could be expected to paint the Gaulish Druids as superstitious primitives, given to such deplorable practices as human sacrifice. It was from this that he came to deliver them and bring the fruits of Rome's matchless civilization. It is, as we know, the oldest of imperialism's excuses, employed alike by the British in India and the French in North Africa.

Secondly, the observations made by enemies of one another, especially at the time of actual hostilities, are notoriously unreliable and coloured by the prejudices of the moment. Having come to Gaul with, among other objects, that of extirpating Druidism, it was hardly to be expected that Caesar would have been invited to be guest of honour at the public performance of its rituals.

Lastly, the two initial chapters of *The Conquest* were the kind of mandatory preface all works of this kind were expected to contain so that one cannot be sure whether its author was recording the result of personal research or merely providing his readers with what they expected of him — a description of the people and places in the narrative — without too meticulous consideration of the credentials of his information.

The classical writers actually possessed a source-book on the subject, unfortunately lost to us. This is the fifty-two volume *Histories* of the Syrian Greek, Posidonius, written at the end of the 2nd Century BC. Now Posidonius cannot himself be taken for a totally impartial witness. He was a Stoic philosopher, that is to say a member of that school which believed that truth was available only to those who lived the simple life, free from the enervating luxury and the influence of extraneous ideas which corrupted their own over-civilized society. In writing about the Druids he was simply using them to prove this thesis.

This bias duly discounted, however, Posidonius was an eminent scholar, employing methods of research which could be said to have pioneered those in use by historians today. There had been a Greek colony on the toe of Gaul, at Massilia, now Marseilles, since about the 7th Century BC. Not only did Gauls and Massiliots have long-standing trade relations, but the Greeks had been so emulated by their neighbours that one writer was moved to describe the nearest Gauls as more Greek than the Greeks. By conducting his inquiries here, as well as by travelling extensively through Gaul itself, Posidonius put together what must surely have been the most balanced and complete account of Celtic life, including its religion, ever produced.

Later writers borrowed from him freely, and it is thanks to this we know of the original work at all. Among them was Strabo (63 BC — AD 21), another Stoic, who had known Posidonius personally; a second was Diodorus of Sicily (circa 40 BC). In his descriptions, Strabo is careful to acknowledge his source. Diodorus, while he fails to do this, often reproduces him almost word for word. It is possible, therefore, to trace the influence of the earlier writer on both.

But what is germane to us is that Caesar has also used Posidonius. For example, the description of the man-shaped wicker colossi in which sacrificial victims were burnt is Strabo verbatim. In other passages, however, since we do not have the original work, it is impossible always to know where Caesar was plagiarizing, where using information of his own. Hence, three of his most important statements stand uncorroborated by other writers and are open to doubt and debate. The first of these is the description of the annual assembly organized by the Druids in the territory of the Carnutes, regarded as the centre of Gaul; the second is his declaration that the Gaulish Druids were subject to a single overriding authority, a kind of "Archdruid", as he has been called; and the third, the statement that the doctrines of Druidism originated in Britain. In assessing these it is necessary to consider other, circumstantial evidence.

With Strabo and Diodorus, Caesar is one of the tiny group of writers whose work is extant and who were alive at the time the Druids were openly practising. There are two others, one of whom is Cicero, contemporary and one-time friend of Caesar's. He claimed actually to have met a Druid in the shape of Divicacus, chief of the Aedui, who sought Rome's assistance against the Helvetii, thus precipitating the Gallic war. Some scholars argue that Cicero was mistaken and that Diviciacus was not a Druid. Error seems unlikely, however, unless the visitor purposely set out to deceive, and such a deception would have been pointless as it would quickly have been discovered if his embassy had succeeded.

What is plain is that the Roman orator and statesman was deeply impressed, perhaps a little too deeply for his judgment to be quite sound. He attributes to Diviciacus "that knowledge of nature which the Greeks call 'Physiologia' " by which he means natural science. But what was it he exalted by this name? Was it, as some scholars hold, little more than that nature- and herb-lore which Pliny shows the Druids to have possessed?

In any case, this kind of idealizing gets scant support from the only other eye-witness, Tacitus, who is the only one to give us any direct information about Druidism in Britain, but who saw it only from the point of view of the forces which had come to destroy it.

For him the Druids are ignorant savages who "deemed it indeed a duty to cover their altars with the blood of captives and to consult their deities through human entrails". This forms part of the passage in the *Annals* in which he describes the terrifying scene confronting the Roman troops attempting to take Anglesey: the "dense array of armed warriors"; the women in black, dashing between the ranks "like the Furies", hair dishevelled and waving brands; the Druids with uplifted hands "pouring forth dreadful imprecations". For all that he is a key observer, one must take into consideration his unconcealed prejudice. He fully accepted the pleas of Roman imperialism and was at pains to make clear to his readers what benefits the conquerors were conferring on "the poor, benighted heathen".

Outside this tiny band we are left with those writers who, on the whole, are merely recycling old facts and offering conclusions about the Druids which become more extravagantly idealized as the distance in time separates them, though, it is true, occasionally providing some new detail verifiable by the light of other data. Lucan, who lived from AD 39 to 65 and, therefore, at a time when at least some first hand witnesses were about, describes the Druids in his epic poem *Pharsalia* as having their abode in "the innermost groves of far-off forests". He may well have heard of the celebrated Druids' grove near the Greek colony of Massilia, always considered to be of great antiquity, and, of course, he corroborates Pliny. The Medieval Berne *Scholiasts* who annotated the *Pharsalia*, provide some additional information, including the names of some gods like Esus, Teutatis and Taranis, known from other sources and it is conceivable that they may have been working from some earlier now lost work, possibly Posidonius.

Valerius Maximus, who wrote a book of anecdotes principally intended to be of assistance to orators, and who lived in the times of Tiberius, himself responsible for the ban on Druidism, mentions the curious custom among the Gauls whereby money lent was made repayable beyond the grave. This links with Diodorus' statement about letters being sent to the dead.

Diogenes Laertius, already mentioned, wrote *The Lives and Opinions of the Eminent Philosophers* in Greek. The prologue begins: "There are some who say that the study of philosophy had its beginnings among the barbarians" and he summons in support the Magi of the Persians, the Chaldeans of the Babylonians and Assyrians, and an Indian caste he calls the "Gymnosophists". He then tells us that "among the Celts and Gauls there are people called Druids or Holy Ones". As his authority he cites the *Magicus*, a lost work by Aristotle, who had lived between 384-322 BC, and Sotion of Alexandria in the twenty-third book of his *Succession of the Philosophers*.

About 390 AD, Ammianus Marcellus wrote a continuation of the *Histories* of Tacitus, using Latin, though his native tongue was Greek. As his source in references to the Celts, he cites Timagenes, a Greek historian of the 1st Century BC and the author of a history of the Gauls also now lost. Ammianus, himself a meticulous and painstaking historian, says of Timagenes that he was "a true Greek in accuracy as well as language" and that he had collected out of the various books those facts long unknown. For his part, however, Ammianus merely recapitulates Strabo, though he does introduce the name of Pythagoras, inferring that he was the initiator of the Druidic doctrine of metempsychosis or transmigration of the soul. The Druids were, he informs us, "bound together in a fraternal organization, as the authority of Pythagoras determined". The mention of an organization might seem like confirmation of Caesar's statements about the annual Druidic convocation in the territory of the Carnutes and the existence of an Archdruid — one would expect such an organized body to have its annual general meeting and its chairman. But the suggestion that the Druids were mere disciples of Pythagoras is so fantastical that the entire passage becomes dubious.

Nevertheless, the Pythagorean link is one pursued by others. In the view of most contemporary scholars it had its origin in the coincidence that both Druids and Pythagoras believed in metempsychosis, though a writer before Ammianus explains it by declaring that the Greek mathematician's mentor was an Assyrian named Nazaratus and that he had himself studied the teachings of the Galatae and the Brahmins. The Brahmins are, of course, a caste of Hindu religious teachers, but

"Galatae" means simply "Gauls" so that one has to assume that what he really intended was that Pythagoras studied the teachings of the "Brahmins and Druids", which might well have been true. And the fact is that the Brahmins, also, believe in and teach metempsychosis.

Hippolytus, writing in his *Philosophoumena*, about the 3rd Century AD, asserts that philosophy, "a science of the highest utility", flourished among the ancient barbarians, and only from them arrived in Greece. His list of those he regards as the precursors of Greek philosophy include not only the Druids of the Gauls and "the Philosophers of the Kelts", a curious distinction, but most of those earlier listed by Diogenes.

Perhaps it was sheer patriotism which led later Greeks to reverse previous trends and restore Pythagoras as instructor of the Druids. For by the time of Cyril of Alexandria in the 4th Century AD, we have the Greek master's Thracian slave, Zalmoxis, as missionary to the Gauls. In any event, the association of Druids and Pythagoras is one which shows considerable persistence, a fact which, of itself, leads one to wonder if it can be totally without foundation. Can this possibly mean that Pythagorean mathematics had a Druidic base? Incredibly the idea is less far-fetched now than it once seemed.

There are four further references to the Druids which though of extremely late date speak of them as if they were still in existence. The *Historia Augusta* is a series of somewhat journalistic biographies of the Roman emperors from Hadrian to Numerianus, covering a period from AD 117 to 284. In the life of Numerianus, we are told that once, when Diocletian, then a young subaltern, was staying in Gaul, his hostess chided him with parsimony. He answered jestingly that he would be more generous once he became emperor — an office which he can at that time have had no hope of attaining. The woman told him not to mock, "For," she said, "when you have killed The Boar, you will indeed be emperor". From then on though he missed no opportunity of killing boars when hunting, he came no nearer to the purple. At last, he killed the prefect Arrius, surnamed The Boar, and was made emperor. What turns this anecdote of fortune-telling into a curiosity is that his hostess, presumably an innkeeper, is described as a "Druidess".

From the life of Aurelianus, also in the *Historia Augusta*, we are told that that emperor was in the habit of consulting "the Gaulish Druidesses" to find out if the imperial diadem would remain in his family's keeping.

And in a third story from the same source we learn that when the emperor, Severus, was on his way to engage the Germans who, in AD 235, were laying Gaul waste, a Druidess called out to him, "Go forward, but hope not for victory, nor put trust in thy soldiers". In fact he was assassinated by mutinous troops and hence won no victory.

The usual explanation of these late relics is that by this time Druidism had degenerated into mere fortune-telling, herbalism and folk-medicine. In any case, it is pointed out, there is no evidence of Druidesses among the earlier writers.

But there may be more to it than this and it is here that the two other sources are relevant. Decimus Magnus Ausonius was born in Bordeaux in AD 310, and subsequently became tutor to the son of the Emperor Valentinian. Before his elevation he had been teacher of rhetoric at the University of Bordeaux, as well as a somewhat idiosyncratic versifier who found his inspiration in such subjects as the months of the year, his own ancestry or, as in this case, his fellow-professors. Of one, whose name he gives as Phoebicius, he writes that he had been keeper of the temple of Belenos and came from the stock of the Druids of Armorica. In an early specimen of academic bitchiness, he adds that getting no profit from his sacerdotal appointment, Phoebicius used the good offices of his son to obtain a chair at the university. The fascinating point is, however, that here we have Druids mentioned some 350 years after the Roman conquest of Gaul and their supposed disappearance.

Since the classical sources are so niggardly of information regarding Druidism we must obviously try to fill the numerous gaps from elsewhere.

The obvious place is archaeology, but, in spite of all the jokes about finds labelled "Cult Object" which have later turned out to be some ordinary domestic utensil, religion is precisely the sphere which finds archaeologists at their most reticent. All too often the "Cult Object" is precisely equivalent to a domestic article. The chalice and paten of the Christian communion are ready examples: the one is goblet, the other a plate and they could as easily occupy a dining table as an altar. The cauldron of the Druids is a similar case, and not even the sacrificial knife necessarily has anything to distinguish it from the common or kitchen variety.

Under certain circumstances, to be sure, the archaeologist, coming on a hoard of objects, perhaps at the bottom of a lake, may be confident enough to pronounce it a votive deposit; or finding a building, declare it a temple.

But, then, did the Druids worship in temples? In general, almost certainly not. Their rites were conducted in the open, in oak groves. And although Diodorus of Sicily, Suetonius and Polybius all speak of "temples and sanctuaries", they may well have been writing in a more or less figurative sense. Certainly many of the buildings identified as Celtic temples or shrines are post-Roman. Nevertheless, in some cases traces of earlier buildings have been found beneath them. Examples are the sites at Mouriés, Saint Blaise and St Germain-les-Rocheux in France; at Schleidweiler in Germany; at Worth and possibly Harlow and Woodeaton in Britain.

A particularly well-known sanctuary at Roquepertuse in France includes niches cut into its stonework to accommodate severed heads, and this feature has been found, among other places, at St Remy-en-Provence, at Entremont, at Mouriés itself and in hill-forts in Britain and elsewhere.

The thesis that any or all of these buildings is actually Druidic rests to some extent on assumption. The sanctuary buildings may have been devoted exclusively to tribal gods whose mediators were the chieftains. In other cases it is not indisputably certain that the buildings were actually temples of any kind. They could have been used for totally secular purposes, as barns or storage places, for example.

And more congruous with known Druidic practice than roofed-in temples and shrines are the open enclosures, surrounded by a ditch or the traces of a palisade, which have been found in many parts of the Celtic world. In area these vary from a few square metres to several hundred and are more commonly rectangular though circular ones are also known. An example is the "Banqueting Hall" on the Hill of Tara in Meath, Ireland.

In some of them bones, both human and animal, have been discovered and may well be the remains of sacrifice. In one case, at Holzhausen in Germany, three shafts were found within the enclosure. In one there was an upright stake and in the surrounding material are organic traces such as might have been left by human or animal flesh. Similar votive shafts have been found in other places — there is a well-known trio of them at La Vendée in France. They have yielded pottery, carved figures, human and animal bones and, in one, a four-metre high cypress.

Some, though by no means all, may at one stage have functioned as wells. This would be consistent with the Druidic belief in an Other World beneath the earth's surface, accessible by way of its waters, itself supported archaeologically by the discovery of votive deposits under the water, such as at La Tène, Llyn Cerrig Bach in Anglesey and in many other places. In any event, whether or not they had been wells, these ritual shafts are very characteristic of Druidic practice.

The so-called Coligny calendar found near Bourg-en-Bresse in the last century and thought to date from the 1st Century BC, confirms that the Druids were calendarists and that they based their calculations on a nineteen-year cycle as a means of reconciling lunar and solar years.

But perhaps most important of all the archaeological discoveries is the great cauldron found at Gundestrup in Denmark in 1880. There are frequent references to cauldrons in Celtic mythology, usually in connexion with the notion of regeneration. They occur twice in the Welsh legends and in both cases describe cauldrons in which the dead are immersed to be restored to life.

There can be no doubt about the sacerdotal purpose of the Gundestrup cauldron, for it is decorated with repoussé-work representations of Celtic gods on silver panels. Some are mere portraits, others full length. Each is associated with animals or humans and sometimes both. One, for instance, is plainly the horned-god, Cernunnos, holding a torc in one hand and a ram-headed serpent, his most common attribute, in the other. He is seated in a Buddha-like, cross-legged position, a posture often seen in Celtic figures and described by Posidonius as the one normally adopted when sitting to eat.

Another plate shows a giant figure grasping by the ankles an infinitely smaller one, whom he is about to immerse head first, in a cauldron or as some authorities have it, into the opening of a ritual shaft: a scene, then, of human sacrifice with the sacrificer here a god. And drowning is known to be one of the modes of sacrifice used by the Druids.

Strabo mentions the Cimbri, a Celticized people inhabiting Jutland, the area in which the Gundestrup Cauldron was found, giving such an object to Caesar Augustus. It is described as the "dearest and most precious" of their possessions and in the same passage the author refers to a form of sacrifice involving a cauldron carried out by the priestesses of the Cimbri. We also know of a giant cauldron, over a metre and half high, called The Crater, which is of Scythian provenance. The Celts probably derived the practice of human sacrifice from the Scythians and the Crater makes it seem likely that they carried out cauldron sacrifices. It certainly corresponds very closely with the kind of enormous vessel Strabo mentions in his account of the Cimbric practices.

At the same time, when one takes the scene on the Gundestrupp Cauldron in conjunction with the legends of warriors brought back to life through immersion in a magic cauldron, one is left wondering whether this is not what is actually being portrayed here and whether the smaller figure is not really a corpse, perhaps fallen in battle, especially as the other figures on the same plate are warriors. Is this, in other words, a portrayal of regeneration through divine intervention?

Of the rest of the archaeological material, human remains under buildings of Celtic date connect with the known Druidic practice, continued into late times, of burying a sacrificial victim to ensure the permanence of new buildings, but others are more doubtful. In 1834 an oak coffin was recovered from a tumulus at Gristhorpe, near Scarborough. Within it was the skeleton of an old man, together with a bronze dagger and various flint instruments. The coffin was itself covered with oak branches and in it were the remains of some foliage, identified at the time as mistletoe. Burial in a tumulus accords with Druidic practice and the presence of mistletoe could be taken as substantial proof of origin. Unfortunately, a great deal of doubt surrounds the entire discovery, including the identification of the foliage, and it cannot be taken at face value.

At Port St Mary in the Isle of Man is a four-foot high sandstone slab dating from about the 5th or 6th Centuries AD. Its inscription is in Ogham characters, a form of runic or linear script used principally in Ireland and confined to epigraphy (though Robert Graves suggests it was also a means of secret communication among the Druids). It has been read as: Dovaidona Maqi Droata, and this translated would mean: Dovadona, Son of the Druid.

This, in the broadest terms, is the sum of archaeological knowledge of the Druids. But there remain two admittedly more problematical sources: one, the so-called vernacular texts; the other, the existing survivals of customs whose origins can be traced back to pagan Celtic times, some of which we discussed in the second chapter of this book.

The texts comprise a series of stories originally without doubt transmitted orally and only at a very late date committed to writing. The older and probably, therefore, more reliable are the Irish ones whose written form dates from the 8th Century AD on; the Welsh stories were in the main transcribed only in Medieval times so that besides undergoing the corruption of time they were also subjected to other literary influences in particular French ones.

Professor Ross hints at a third repository of vernacular material, as yet unpublished, in the traditional oral literature of the Scottish Highlands. These are later still: indeed many did not achieve written form until our own times when folklorists were able to persuade the story-tellers to recite their repertories into the microphones of tape-recorders. Although they contain references to Celtic gods and known practices, these have become inextricably confused with later Christian legends and with events in Scottish history down the centuries.

Whether Irish, Welsh or Scottish, the stories are in epic form and, superficially, are the description of intertribal and dynastic quarrels, conquests and invasions, occasionally with a kernel of known history beneath the thick husk of legend.

At the same time, they are replete with creatures — bulls, boars, salmon, eagles, ravens — with supernatural powers whose existence we can trace back through the layers of Celtic prehistory, and with known customs and references to gods. Unrecognized as such by the Medieval scribes who wrote the stories down, however, these last now stand on terms of parity with the human characters and often play subsidiary roles. Thus, in *How Culhwch Won Olwen*, one of the earliest stories in which King Arthur figures, one character, Mabon ap Modron (the name means, Son, Son of Mother) is undoubtedly the deity, Maponos, whose name also means "Son" or "Divine Son". He is to be found on five dedications in the north of England and is recalled in two place-names, Lochmaben and Clochmabenstane in Dumfriesshire.

The "divine son" who is abducted and taken to the Other World, finally to be rescued, is a fundamental myth found in most agricultural societies and personifies the cycle of seedtime and harvest. In four of the dedications, which are Gallo-Roman, Maponos is equated with Apollo and one of these, a partially-defaced altar stone found at Ribchester, Lancashire, originally had four figures, of which two are of goddesses, interpreted as huntresses. In one of the best known versions of the "abducted divine son" myth, that of Adonis, the god is wounded in a boar-hunt. Mabon, who in the story has also been abducted, participates after his rescue, in a hunt for the supernatural boar, Twrc Trywth.

The Celtic god most often regarded as the equivalent of Apollo is the sun-god, Belenos. But if one follows the genealogy of the "divine son" further back one finds that he, too, was a sun-god, as in the case of the Egyptian Horus, son of Isis. Can it be, then, that Maponos is simply the sun-god Belenos designated by some other name, and that here we have the vestiges of a Celtic "abducted divine son" myth?

This is not, by any means, the only case of such hints' being left hanging tantalizingly in mid-air. In the Welsh *mabinogi* of *Pwyll Lord of Dyved*, there is another. In one incident in the story, Teirnon Twrvliant has a succession of foals stolen each May Eve (the Celtic festival of Beltain). Finally, he decides to keep watch over his mare and, as she delivers, a huge claw comes in through the window and grabs the new-born animal. Teirnon slices the claw from its arm with his sword and rushes outside, but all he finds is a babe in silk swaddling bands. The child turns out to be the stolen son of the queen, Rhiannon. Another thread is pursued, however, and so we never return to this intriguing theme to discover who is the owner of the giant claw. The story-teller is obviously unaware of much significant detail: that, for example, Rhiannon is the Welsh form of the great horse-goddess Epona, known right across the Celtic world. This must have been the connexion with foaling mares—a theme also abandoned.

For all this, the stories constantly reiterate important pagan Celtic themes. There is, for example, the struggle between an older man (often the father) and a younger man for a woman. The cost of the younger man's victory is, invariably, the sexual virility of the older one. This occurs in both the stories just mentioned and altogether no fewer than seven times in the Welsh *mabinogi* legends. Jeffrey Gantz, editor of the Penguin edition of them suggests it can be taken to represent spring, the woman, and summer, the young man, in conflict with a god governing winter.

There are in these stories too accounts of those visits to the Other World to wrest from its guardians some magical treasure beneficial or essential to humanity. This illustrates that movement between the two planes of existence always easily made in Celtic myth, especially during the season of Samain. Lastly, there is the notion of the violated or abducted queen, without doubt a mother-goddess whose absence spells disaster for her people and who must accordingly be rescued.

As leads in a search for the Druids, one cannot rely on the myths as we now have them to provide unsupported evidence though they often give useful confirmation and elucidation of data coming from other sources. And what is perhaps more important, they often evoke the atmosphere of the Celtic supernatural with that mysterious interlocking of the living and the dead through the tremendous powers latent in the natural environment.

The same caution also applies in assessing surviving and recently abandoned folk-customs; nonetheless they do give us some idea of the spread of pagan Celtic festivals and hence of the deities which these celebrated. The horned god is a case in point, since it seems a reasonable conjecture that customs like the Abbots Bromley stag-dance and the *Pardon* St Cornely must commemorate him.

But it can also suggest leads to be followed up. We know, for example, that both prophecy and herb-medicine are practised by latterday "wise men" and "wise women". This might well cause us to consider whether the Druids also practised these arts, as of course we know they did. Similarly, water-divining or "dowsing" is also associated with "wise" men and women, indeed the French word *sorcier* means, literally, "one who finds sources"—in other words, a water-diviner. This provokes the question: did the Druids practise it?

CHAPTER FIVE

An Ancestry Of Druidism

IN the descriptions of the Druids among those classical writers who can be taken as contemporary with them there is a singular omission. While most standard reference works speak of them as "priests of the Celts", none of the Posidonian sources so describes them.

Caesar says that they were "occupied about things divine, they carry out sacrifice—public and private, and interpret religious matters" ("... ulli rebus divinis intersunt, sacrificia publica ac privata procurant, religionem interpretantur"). Pliny writes of "magicians" and in so far as he defines this further it is as "diviners and physicians", the latter word chiming with his description of their practice of herbalism. Among the others: to Strabo they are "natural and moral philosophers"; to Diodorus "philosophers" versed in religious affairs; and to Diogenes Laertius, quoting Aristotle and Sotion, "philosophers", without qualification.

Since each of these writers was, in his own way, endeavouring to interpret the Druids to those presumed to be ignorant of them, it is surely a little strange that none made the one comparison likely to render them immediately understandable: that between the priests with whom their readers were familiar, and those of the Celts. In other contexts, alien sacerdotal bodies are quite freely, even wantonly, translated so. Titus Livy, for example, uses the expression *antistites templi* to describe a foreign priesthood; a Gallo-Roman inscription at Arles gives the feminine form, *anti stitia deae*, while another at Antibes records a *flaminica sacerdos* serving the goddess Thucolis, notwithstanding the fact that the *flamens* were a specifically Roman body. Even Caesar, who himself bore the sacerdotal title of *pontifex maximus* and who glosses Celtic gods with Roman ones, does not describe the Druids by any word approximating in meaning to "priest".

The most obvious explanation is that the Druids were so unlike what these writers understood a priest to be that the term appeared quite inappropriate. But it could have been that there was, in addition, a totally different body recognizably functioning as a priesthood as they understood it.

If this was the case, why do we know so little of it? The first part of the answer lies in the mental attitude of the observers themselves. Despite the admirable opportunities available to them, neither Greeks nor Romans showed any inclination towards the study of comparative religion. The fact was that they saw the beliefs of most of the subject peoples as only an unrefined version of their own—which to some extent they were. To be worthy of comment, the manifestations of a religion had to be both different and dramatic. Druidism succeeded in both respects.

The second part of the answer is that other religious leaders among the Celts are recorded, though by little more than intimation. Diogenes Laertius, for example, mentions "druidae" and "semnotheoi". The second word is totally mysterious and without any agreed interpretation, though the suffix "-theoi" means "gods".

There were in addition various bodies of priestesses, like those of the Cimbri described by Strabo. He mentions also a body of women practising on an offshore island of Gaul, which may be one of the Channel Islands. They were, he says, devoted to a Dionysian cult whose rituals included an annual rethatching of their temple in a single day. If, in the process, one of their number had the misfortune to stumble and drop her load she was set on by the rest and torn to pieces. The victim was, he assures us, always settled on in advance and a means found of tripping her.

Besides these, there are the accounts of tribal leaders performing sacrifice. One is Queen Boudicca offering women to her victory-goddess, Adraste, after her defeat of the Romans. The other is Queen Cartimandua, ruler of the Brigantes, who invokes the goddess Brigid or Brigantia.

More promising than such random and casual instances, however, is the Celtic title *gutuater*, found on four inscriptions and twice mentioned by Caesar. These two references occur in the Eighth Book of *The*

Conquest of Gaul, which was written not by Caesar but by his friend Hirtius. Here the word appears to be used as a proper name, but it is generally held that this was an error and that it actually refers to a man who held the rank of *gutuater*. As Kendrick points out, he was plainly not a Druid, since while both Caesar and Hirtius were obviously confused about what a *gutuater* was, they knew perfectly well what a Druid was and would, therefore, have so described him had he been one.

The word has been variously translated as "master" or "father of invocation" (of prayer) or just as "the Invoker". It may be, as some scholars hold, that the *gutuater* represented a grade of priesthood, in other words some kind of 'curate' Druid, but if this is so we have no mention of them as such. In any case, the various renderings of the word actually makes them sound more like priests than any of the definitions of the word Druid ("wise man", "wise man of the oak", "man of great wisdom" to quote a few). And invocation or prayer is nearer to a priestly function than most of those ascribed to the Druids, though one must bear in mind that Diogenes Laertius says they were called "Druids or Holy Ones".

But perhaps it is here—with definitions—that we should begin: if we can find an acceptable definition for the word "priest" we can then decide whether the Druids come within its ambit. In essence, it can, I think, be agreed that a priest is "one who acts as mediator between a community and its deities". The concept of deities itself represents, as we know, an advanced stage in cultural development. Gods have personalities, are capable of being pleased and displeased and so there stems from them the notions leading to the development of morality and religious ethics. Initially, however, what is likely to exercise their worshippers is less abstractions of this kind than the manifest power of the gods to harm or benefit mortals. For are they not masters of the elements; commanders of sun, moon, tides, seasons; lords of life and death? Accordingly, the only person equipped to mediate with them must be the most powerful of mortals—the tribal chief. And as the tribe is subsumed into nation, the king will succeed to the function.

The hypothesis is confirmed by the evidence. With the Egyptians, for instance, the pharoah was also high priest. A drawing of King Ay, predecessor of Tutankhamen, shows him in his ritual garb. If one takes the Hittites, first of the great Indo-European civilizations, for whom nationhood came late in their history, one finds a similar state of affairs, saving that beside the national deities there still remained a large pantheon of local, formerly tribal ones, and among the priest-king's duties was that of making an annual tour of their shrines to render tribute.

That the Celtic chieftain, at any rate in late time, fulfilled the sacerdotal role is obvious from the instances of Boudicca and Cartimandua.

The Egyptian word usually translated as "priest" means strictly

"Servants of the Gods" and we know they were restricted to the menial, quotidian tasks of the temple. The Roman pontifices, for all they were often patricians, were also originally appointed to carry out the more or less routine liturgical functions, the main ones belonging to the kings up till republican times whereafter they were largely secularized to become sinecures.

What emerges, therefore, is that on the whole priests as the ancient world understood them fulfilled a secondary rather than a primary religious function. But the classical sources are virtually unanimous in pronouncing the Druids supreme in Celtic religion. In any case, the order displays an independence and superiority which makes it inconceivable that they can have been mere royal appointees. The king was not, for example, permitted to speak until his Druids had first expressed their opinions. In *The Cattle Raid of Cooley*, we are told that, "in Ulster no man spoke before Conchobhar, and Conchobhar would not speak before the three Druids".

If the Celts had priests in the sense of secondary religious functionaries, like those of Egypt, Rome and elsewhere, we can declare with some confidence that they could not have been the Druids.

What then were they?

To my mind the most helpful guide towards a definition is the list of "barbarian philosophers" provided by Diogenes Laertius who brackets together Druids, the Persian Magi, the "Chaldeans" of the Babylonians and Assyrians, and the body he calls the "Gymnosophists" of the Hindus. Why of all the enormous numbers available did he alight on this four? The vital clue is the inclusion of the Persian Magi, for it is this which shows what unites the names on the list. All were magicians—indeed, the word itself comes from Magi as Aristotle whose *Magicus* provided Diogenes with one of his two sources knew.

And if we exclude the term "Chaldean" we find that they are also united in another way. Druids, Magi and "Gymnosophists" all existed among peoples derived from the same racial root-stock, the wandering tribes who were the original inhabitants of Southern Russia—the Indo-Europeans. Their migrations towards Europe, Iran and India could be said to represent the three thrusts of their first expansion, westward, southward and eastward.

And, as a matter of fact, the inclusion of the word "Chaldean" plainly arises from a misapprehension on the part of either Diogenes or his source. It was not the name of any sort of religious body; it was that of the founding race of the Babylonian empire, which, of course, absorbed the Assyrians. In other words, Babylon consisted of the Chaldeans and the Assyrians—Babylonians and Assyrians were not separate peoples as the text implies. The error arose because the priesthood of the Babylonians whose members could with some accuracy be called "magicians"

was largely drawn from the Chaldeans, as was the ruling aristocracy of
the empire. They were, inter alia, pioneers of astrology, astronomy and
mathematics—the Greeks called them *mathematiki*. In late time, however,
they became itinerant astrologers, and frequently turned up in Rome
(though forbidden the city), where they were known as "Chaldeans";
thus the name became synonymous with the practices of astrology,
fortune-telling and associated quasi-magical pursuits.

Though their relevance to Diogenes' list will shortly become clear, for
the moment we can safely ignore them and consider whether it is possible that the migrating Indo-Europeans carried with them a system of
ideas so similar that all qualified for inclusion in a list of what might be
called "pioneer philosophers" drawn up a millennium later. But let us
first be clear what was meant by "philosophy". To Greeks like Aristotle
or Diogenes, as to 18th Century Europeans, it signified as much a preoccupation with the natural world as with pure metaphysical speculation.
Newton was no less a philosopher in these terms than Hume, and was so
described. And our own universities, after all, still make our post-
graduate scientists Doctors of Philosophy. Astronomy, even under the
guise of astrology, calendary, mathematics, herbalism, as well as those
sheer speculations "about the heavenly bodies and their movements", to
which, according to Caesar, the Druids were so much addicted, would
all come under the heading of "Philosophy" to Aristotle or Diogenes.

As it happens one of the three bodies on the latter's list has survived.
The Indo-European migrants who, about the beginning of the 15th
Century BC, reached India were the "Aryan" invaders, founders of
Hinduism. There are numerous startling resemblances between Hinduism and Druidism. Both practised cremation of the dead, carried out
human sacrifice, had vast numbers of deities and taught metempsychosis. (The similarities actually go down to quite trifling detail:
Buddha is normally depicted as sitting in the same cross-legged position
the Celts are described as adopting and in which their gods are often
shown.)

But there had emerged in Hinduism, as its intellectual leadership, the
Brahmins: these must be Diogenes' "Gymnosophists". The late Myles
Dillon, Professor of Celtic Studies at the University of Dublin, has drawn
up a list of the similarities between Brahmins and Druids. He points out
that, for example, they were highest caste of a four-caste system, with the
knights or *Kshatriyas* coming next below them. Caesar declares that the
Druids and the knights were the two most highly esteemed classes in
Gaulish society. He does not actually give one or other precedence,
though he describes the Druids first and begins the next section with the
words "The second class is that of the Knights ..."

The Brahmins, like the Druids, were communal lawgivers. Both recognized either forms of marriage. Of the Brahmins, Max Weber says

that they occupied the positions of princely-chaplains, and acted as counsellors and as theological teachers. They were to be found as singers of epics extolling the heroic and deriding the unworthy. All were functions of the Druids.

Like Druidic doctrine, that of the Brahmins was originally transmitted by word of mouth. Weber points out that even when it came to be written down it still plainly exhibited that it had been fashioned for easy memorization and reproduction. Extensive use was made of plays on words, epigrams, aphorisms, verse and recurring refrains of the "This-is-the-house-that Jack-built" type.

Most importantly, both acted as advisers on ritual, placing great emphasis on its correct execution.

The similarities are such that one might suppose that Brahmins and Druids had been in contact, but as this is inconceivable, the only answer is that both developed out of an earlier, parent body.

We might suppose that they encountered this in their original Indo-European homelands, which must have been not only a racial nursery, but also the place where the stirrings of an apprehension of the supernatural occurred. According to Father William Schmidt who in 1931 produced his magnum opus, *The Origins of the Idea of God*, the first signs of this are those pre-hunt rituals whose aim is not merely to ensure mastery over the prey, but also to allay the anger of its "spirit". He gives a typical example from anthropology and describes a pygmy-artist drawing a representation of his quarry before pursuing it. Afterwards, having been successful, he puts blood and hair from the slaughtered animal on his picture, then rubs out the entirety as the rising sun touches it. The cave painters, such as those of Lascaux with their scenes of hunters and prey must certainly have had similar intentions.

This concern with the wrathful spirits of the dead forms not only an initial, but a constant manifestation of the notion of the supernatural among early peoples. Everything possesses a soul—not just such animate things as humans, animals, fish, plants, but also the apparently inanimate, stones, earth, water, wood. As an Eskimo told the Danish explorer Rasmussen in 1929, it was in this that the greatest threat to humanity lay. "All those we have to strike down ... have souls, as we have," he pointed out, "souls that do not perish with the body and which therefore must be propitiated lest they revenge themselves on us for taking away their bodies."

What first changes is that stage at which the propitiatory rituals are carried out by each or any member of the group of hunters. It gives place to one wherein, the social units having increased in size and complexity, this becomes the responsibility of an expert. He is the shaman, able to throw himself into trances in which he can enter the Land of the Spirits, communicate with its inhabitants and hence on his return dictate the rituals necessary not merely to banish those which are malign causing illness or other misfortunes, but also with the help of his personal tutelary spirits to invoke the aid of others both powerful and well-disposed.

The word "shaman" is derived from the language of the Tungus peoples of Siberia, among whom he is still to be found practising, as he is among the nomadic herdsmen and hunters of northern Europe, the Arctic and the plains of north-east Asia. But under a score of different names he is to be found all over the world in rural communities living by hunting and fishing, with at best a little subsistence farming or nomadic pastoralism. His reputation, however, may well spread beyond the confines of his native village. The witch-doctor, the *obeahs* of the Caribbean, the Voodoo-priests of Haiti and West Africa, the Candomblés of Brazil, all have among their patrons and membership of their cult-groups sophisticated and often well-educated town-dwellers.

More than anyone, the shaman can claim to a vocation: that it is shamanism that chooses him, not he it. Impelled by some power he cannot resist, often a succession of dreams, he withdraws from the society of his fellows to live in the wild, where, fasting and meditating, he lays himself open as it were to the very forces immanent in his natural surroundings.

Soon he will become prey to terrible visitations. He may believe himself to be undergoing many incarnations in the space of a few nights, culminating in some dreadful act of symbolical self-immolation. At last he will reach stasis and his own ultimate reward—a total union with the Cosmos. As well as the spirits of the dead, he will have emerged from his trauma in touch with "all the spirits of earth and sky and sea" in the words of Rasmussen's informant who was himself a shaman. From now on all these will be his guides and helpers.

Thus reborn, his first companions will be other shamans who recognize him as one fit to share their secrets: those of animal and bird life; of cloud and climate; stars and their motions; herbs and their properties. But above all, he will learn the great myths which are the history of his people.

When he returns to the midst of his fellow men, probably under a new name as token of his regeneration, they will quickly recognize that he is a different person, the recipient of special wisdom. At one with nature and the elements, he may now choose for his habitat some remote place in the forest and it is here he will have to be sought for consultation.

The intimacy of his union with nature will be demonstrated by his very costume, so that when he wishes to commune with bird-spirits he will wear a dress of feathers; to reach animal-spirits he will wear skins or adorn himself with horns or antlers; when it is the spirits of tree or plant life he seeks he will don the green of foliage or the colours of flowers or fruit. He has become, one would say, a magician—the word the classical writers most frequently use in describing the Druids.

Certainly in shamanism we have a system of belief whose lineage stretches back perhaps 20,000 years. Something very close to it existed among the inhabitants of Scandinavia as early as Neolithic times. Its effect on the Druids is obvious and it is virtually certain that there were shamans among the Indo-Europeans before the great migrations.

On the other hand, if the Druids had developed out of what had been the common heritage of the Indo-Europeans, why should the practices of the Magi, the Brahmins and the Druids have excited the comment of Greek observers, themselves Indo-Europeans? And it is surely unlikely that they would have attributed the foundation of philosophy, of which the Greeks were so proud, to these quite alien bodies unless there was good reason for their doing so. How, in any case, does one account for the presence of the Babylonians on the list, since they were not Indo-Europeans?

The truth is that there may well have been another shamanic body, infinitely more highly developed than the normal run or, indeed, than most contemporary shamans as they have been encountered by anthropologists. We might call them the "super-shamans".

Their trail can be followed by the clear imprints they have left behind. One of these which Geoffrey Ashe pursues at length is the universality of the "sacred heptad", the number seven: seven days of the week; Seven Deadly Sins; seven planets; seven metals of alchemy; Seven Pillars of Wisdom; seven seas; the seven-tiered Ziggurat of Babylon; the seven-branched candelabra of the Jewish temple—and the list can be extended still further.

In almost every instance the choice of the number is arbitrary and can be explained only by attaching an occult significance to it. This is probably an association with astrology so that it represents either the seven planets or (as Geoffrey Ashe argues) the seven stars of the Great Bear. With astrology or astronomy must go mathematics, without which calendration, which is one of their practical fruits or, for that matter horoscope casting, is impossible. We can conclude, therefore, the super-shamans were also astronomers and mathematicians.

Eliade has pointed out another clue to his presence: the importance of the "Cosmic Centre". This has nothing to do with purely geometrical centres, but relates to the belief that there are special centres at which the powers of the supernatural are greatest. Typically they take the form of a mountain, like Mount Zion, or a tree, of which the Norse World Tree, Yggdrasil, is a good example. Both may take symbolical form. The Ziggurat was a symbolical mountain connecting heaven, earth and underworld, and the ascent of a symbolical tree formed and still forms part of the ritual of central and north Asiatic shamans.

With these and other clues we can trace the influence of the super-shaman on many of the world's great religions. Its ideas crossed the Bering Straits to reach those of the civilizations of Central and South America probably no later than 10,000 BC. It plainly influenced Babylon and the other Semitic religions. It underlies Chinese Taoism, as well as Tibetan Buddhism. And is it not significant that in his search for "enlightenment", Gautama Buddha, himself an Indo-European, chose the traditional shamanic way of withdrawal from society and solitary meditation in the wilderness?

If we return to Diogenes' list and look for connexions with the super-shamans we find that Magi, Brahmins, Babylonian priests and Druids were all astrologers, mathematicians and calendarists. The Babylonian priests were, indeed, pre-eminent in these fields, and are credited with the introduction of concepts still in use. Their calendar, counted among the world's first accurate ones, was based on the nineteen-year or Metonic cycle. A similar system was used by the Druids. The number seven repeatedly occurs in connexion with all four—the Ziggurat, for example, had seven-tiers.

And if we look at the Brahmins, about whom we are best informed, the coincidences are even more striking. Seven is their mystic number, occurring no fewer than 154 times in the *Rig Veda*, the sacred book of Hinduism. They were both astrologers and mathematicians and they showed a special preoccupation with the "Cosmic Centre" so that in the invocations which accompany the felling of the tree to be used as a sacrificial stake, it is addressed as the link between earth, air and heaven—a concept very similar to the Babylonian.

Their main function was that of ritual advisers. They are, as Weber says, "magicians who developed into a hierocratic caste of cultured men".

But perhaps, in passing, we should say something about this very concept of "magician". The word, as used by the classical writers, comes from the Greek "mageia", itself from the Persian word "Magi" and means simply "possessors of wisdom" (as in the Wise Men who visited the Christ-child in Bethlehem). As men of wisdom the Magi commanded the respect of virtually the entire ancient world, including that of the otherwise rather self-satisfied Hebrews. Their astrology had, for example, enabled them to predict that the star seen over Bethlehem portended an important birth. Through their founder, Zoroaster or Zarathustra, they taught what is virtually a montheistic religion of which the tenets were highly influential on others, notably Judaism and Christianity.

It was probably in this sense of wisdom and knowledge, rather than in the accepted later one with which we are familiar that the term "magician" was applied to all three bodies, including the Druids, though it undoubtedly also comprehended the occult skills they were thought to possess.

But, in any event, magic has been of inestimable benefit in the development of science, of which it is the true ancestor, so that mathematics develops from numerology; astronomy from astrology; medicine from magical herbalism; and chemistry from alchemy. But even to say that the "one develops out of the other" is imprecise. In reality they go hand in hand. One cannot, for example, practise numerology without a knowledge of mathematics or astrology without some knowledge of astronomy.

We can say that all four of the bodies listed by Diogenes had been influenced by the super-shamans and that the practices of this body probably included mathematics and astronomy, even if under the guises of numerology and astrology.

But what does not follow is that these contacts were all at first hand. In the case of the Druids it seems to me very probable they were not. They could well have encountered them at second hand. The most likely vehicle of transmission, therefore, would seem to be the Scythians. Originating perhaps in Iran or the Caspian Basin their migrations had brought them into contact with the early Celts in their original Bohemian homeland.

The Scythians practised a form of totemistic shamanism, that is to say they believed themselves to have descended from animal-spirits and they employed shamans to mediate with them. Among the numerous similarities with the Druids were their practices of sacrifice by drowning and their use of a magic wand. According to Markale, the Scythians preferred willow while the Druids chose yew or mountain-ash; in both cases, the wand was an essential tool of prophecy. Both decapitated fallen enemies and believed in metempsychosis, as is evident from their waggon and chariot burials with grave goods including food.

It would be difficult to deny the extent of Scythian influence on the Celts or their religion. On the other hand, the more esoteric reaches of Druidism, those aspects of it which so impressed outsiders, were, I believe, the result of quite different encounters, encounters with a system of beliefs both more potent and much nearer home and these will later be discussed.

CHAPTER SIX

Successors Of The Shamans

CELTIC society was, of course, much more highly developed than that in which shamans are usually found: hunting and pastoralism had given place to farming; metal was mined and worked; there was an external trade. We can hardly expect, in these circumstances, to find shamans as known to contemporary anthropology and the Druids on all fours with one another.

Nonetheless, it is a recognizably shamanistic viewpoint, one which sees human and natural environment as totally interpenetrated which gives Celticism its characteristic ambiance, its special flavour. A breathing vitality sometimes benign, often menacing, charges the landscape and especially those deep, looming forests which must have covered so much of Gaul and the British Isles. The feeling of it is present in their art, in the accurate rendering of leaves, birds or animals; it is present, too, in the Arthurian legends and the earlier myths. The strange giants and other creatures there encountered seem to grow out of woodland itself, to personify it. It is, we might say, the world of nature as apprehended in shamanistic terms, one which can never be seen as deserted because it is peopled by the very things which make it up—rocks, trees, fungi, fern, wild flowers, running stream or spring, even air and cloud, to say nothing of its fauna.

But can we find this shamanistic aspect confirmed elsewhere? Let us take Pliny's archetypal image of the white-robed figures of the mistletoe-culling ceremony. For the ancients mistletoe was a most important plant perhaps because its occurrence as a parasite, growing rootless on trees, lent it a mystery as of something divinely sent. We know that in Norse legend it was a spear of mistletoe which killed Baldr. There was besides, the grove sacred to Diana at Meni: here a runaway slave could obtain his manumission by first plucking a branch of the plant and then killing the priest of the grove, himself an escaped slave, to become his successor.

What is significant to us, however, is that the berry of the mistletoe is white, though as the very title of Frazer's *Golden Bough* reminds us, it gradually turns golden after plucking. In shamanistic terms, these facts alone account for the white worn by the gatherers and for the use of a golden sickle to cut it.

We can suppose, therefore, that a white robe was not so much the regular canonical dress of the Druids, making them look so comfortingly like Church of England clergymen, as the colour appropriate to the particular ceremony. And the passage offers its own confirmation: the bulls sacrificed after the gathering were also white; so was the cloth into which the plant was dropped.

In other words, the Druidic manner of dress derives from the shamanic tradition which suited costume to occasion. The descriptions of Druids given in the Irish myths lend support to this. In one context, a dress of coloured cloak and earrings of gold is mentioned. The great Druid, Mac Roth, is described as putting on the "skin of a hornless, dun-coloured bull" and "a speckled bird headdress" with fluttering wings, as Ross says, a typically shamanistic appearance, but which makes clear that there was no single set of Druidic vestments.

For all this, because of its frequent appearance one may well suppose that white was the most important colour, being derived, perhaps, from a sun or moon deity.

While discussing the question of appearance we might consider another aspect of it which has formed part of the stereotype representation: the full beard. The fact is that while there are, certainly, examples of bearded Celts, a lush moustache was the more normal form of facial adornment. If there was anything which distinguished the Druids facially one might hazard that it would have been a tonsure. The first reference to the ceremonial bestowal of this in Christianity occurs in documents of the Gallicans, the clergy of Gaul before Charlemagne imposed the Roman rule upon it. These early Celtic fathers must certainly have been anxious to prove themselves true successors of the Druids and may well have decided to adopt their distinguishing marks.

In any event, we know that by the 6th Century, the form of the tonsure had become one of the major sources of conflict between the Celtic and Roman Churches. Among the Roman clergy, the so-called tonsure of St Peter had been adopted which, in imitation of the apostle's supposed bald head, consisted of a shaven crown. The Celtic tonsure took the form of a swathe running from ear to ear so that the hairline began at the top of the head, whence it was allowed to grow freely.

The term which Rome used to denounce this is significant: it was declared to be "the tonsure of Simon Magus", the magician mentioned in the Acts of the Apostles, who sought to do a deal with St Peter by which he would have the right to impart the Holy Spirit by the laying on of hands. This, too, is significant, for it shows that Simon was himself involved in a shamanistic cult, spirit-possession being an essential tenet of these. There was an accretion of early Christian legend round his name and he came to be regarded as a sort of primal magician (the name Magus is actually the singular of Magi). Any who practised activities associated with magic, of which consorting with spirits was one, were inevitably dubbed "followers of Simon Magus" by the early church. And among those who were thus denounced were, in point of fact, the Druids.

Also consistent with their shamanic ancestry is the performance of their rituals in the open, in sacred groves, especially those far from centres of population. Although long since abandoned and forgotten in southern Europe, such practices were common enough in the north. Tacitus tells us that the Germans, for example, "consecrated forests and groves, calling by the names of gods that hidden power which they beheld only with the eye of reverence", though we have to bear in mind that the Germans Tacitus was describing were those who had been Celticized. Even today religions dominated by shamans follow such practices. Kendrick points to the Maori of New Zealand as an example.

The Celtic word for a sacred gove, *nemeton*, is cognate with the Latin *nemus*, meaning a clearing in a wood and possibly also with the Greek *tenemos* which, strictly, meant a piece of land apportioned to a god. The word is recurrent in place-names right through the Celtic word. Drunemeton in what was the territory of the Galatians, in Asia Minor, is sometimes taken as evidence that Druidism was to be found as distantly as this. In France, Nanterre comes from Nemetodurum; in Spain there was Nemetobriga; and in the British Isles, Medioneton in Scotland and Vernemeton (Great Grove) which stood between Leicester and Lincoln, and is referred to by Fortunatus in the 6th Century AD. Even Buxton in Derbyshire was originally *Aqua Arnemetiae*, plainly a latinization of an earlier Celtic name. In 11th Century Brittany, there is a reference to a wood called "Nemet" and in Old Irish *nemed* meant a shrine.

There is even a goddess, Nemetona, invoked in Pfalz in Germany and at Bath in Britain.

Lucan, as we know, refers to the well-known grove of oak-trees near Massilia and Pliny tells us that the choice of an oak grove was "for the sake of the trees alone". Maximus of Tyre, who corroborates Lucan, says the oak was the symbol of the Celtic thunder-god to whom he ascribes the Greek name, Zeus. One reason for this association could well be because the oak is particularly prone to being struck by lightning.

Pliny goes still further in linking the Druids with the oak and says the name itself may be derived from the Greek word for the tree, *drus*. Piggott and Powell, among modern writers, generally tend to agree, and define the word roughly as "wise man of the oak" or "one with knowledge of the oak". Ross dismisses both these derivations, though adding that "its exact meaning is in question". Markale, too, disagrees. In his view, the birch and not the oak was the principal sacred tree of Druidism. The word "oak" would hardly figure in their name, therefore, and he suggests it should be understood as "dru-wid-es", "the far-seeing ones" or "the very knowing ones."[1]

But we also know that Druidic practices were associated with sources of water as the entrances to Other Worlds. In the Welsh *mabinogi* of *Branwen Daughter of Llyr*, a huge man emerges from a lake with a cauldron on his back. Similar motifs occur in Arthurian legend, such as the woman's arm which emerges from the lake bearing Arthur's sword, Excalibur. Archaeology confirms the importance of water. In Llyn Cerrig Bach, the lake on the Isle of Anglesey, objects which had come from all parts of Britain have been found. Among metalwork there were slave chains and even complete chariots, deposited in a vain attempt to invoke the aid of the gods against the advancing Romans under Suetonius Paulinus.

Posidonius, cited by Strabo, mentions a "sacred precinct and pool" in a region near Toulouse. Treasure taken from it and later pillaged by the Roman consul Caepio in 102 BC, comprised an estimated 45,000 kilogrammes of gold and nearly 50,000 kilogrammes of silver. Deposits at Coventina's Well, at Carrawborough, Northumberland, included a human skull and several replicas of human heads, as well as 14,000 coins, a bronze dog and horse, glass, ceramics, bells and pins. The custom of dropping pins into sacred or "curative" wells is, of course, still to be found, and this persistence of customs involving waters reappears in other contexts. Gregory of Tours, writing in the 6th Century AD, describes a festival held on the shores of Lake Cevennes in which ani-

---

[1] I am obliged to Margaret Killip of the Manx Museum for a further suggestion. The Manx Celtic word "druaight" means, she tells me, "enchantment". There are similar words in both Scottish and Irish tongues. This would make "Druid" something like "Enchanter", a very fitting title which places them firmly among the magicians and shamans.

mals were sacrificed and offerings hurled into the waters. Meetings continued on this spot until 1868. Parcels have also been seen floating in the waters of the hilltop pool of Dow Loch in Dumfriesshire as late as the present century.

An Other World connected with the mortal one by way of the waters is also inherent in the various representations of aquatic birds, found by archaeologists. The swan, particularly, with its eerie, silent gliding across the face of the water, to say nothing of its majestic grace and beauty, is to be found at the deepest levels of Celtic history, indicating that it was at least one divine creature brought with them on their migrations.

It is also to be found playing the leading part in one of the earliest of the Irish myths, that of Angus, "the young son" of In Dagda, "the good god". Fallen sick with love for a girl he has seen only in a dream, Angus is impelled to seek out the reality and discovers she is actually daughter of Ethal Anbuail, a *sidh*-dweller of Connaught. Angus visits a lake where he is told that the girl is to be found and there sees her, the tallest of a group of 150, "three times fifty", in the usual Celtic phrase. Representations made on his behalf to her father are abortive for he claims that she is under a powerful spell by which she is a woman one year and a swan the next. In order to win her, Angus is told he must copulate with her while she is in swan form and must himself become one for the purpose.

He is told the transformation is due to take place at Samain and going to the lake at the proper time sees the girls have now become 150 swans. He calls to his beloved, is changed into a swan himself and both fly thrice round the lake, chanting music which lulls everyone to sleep for three days and three nights.

Besides the essential role of water and creatures of water in this story, another common Celtic theme is introduced: that of the struggle between an older man (usually the father) and a young one for a woman, representing the conflict between summer and winter. The sleep of three days and three nights may, in these circumstances, represent symbolically the period of winter dormancy, a passage preceding rebirth. This cycle would have been frustrated, we can conclude, had Angus not won his swan-love. There are numerous myths in which the aging of some important being, usually a king, results in the entire sterility of his land.

The association of water-sources and trees as places of special sanctity is present in very many religions. In the Norse with, like Druidism, its strongly shamanistic foundation the gods sit in daily conclave under the World Tree, Yggdrasil, whose trunk and branches reach to the skies to overspread the earth, while of its three roots one reaches down to the world of death, one to that of the frost-giants and the third to that of men. Round its base, however, lie three wells, one of which, Urdar-

brunnr, is that from which the fates, conceived like their Greek counterparts as a feminine trio, plot the course of men's lives. One may, therefore, suspect a common source for these concepts in three Indo-
European religions.

But the tree is also, of course, a centre and one is reminded that
Caesar tells us that the territory of the Carnutes, where the Druids held
their annual convention, was regarded as the epicentre of Gaul. It was
here that, as the gods foregathered under the World Tree, the Druids,
themselves in many ways close to gods, met to pass judgment and to take
their most solemn decisions. This assembly, no doubt itself held under
trees (much of the area was forest), was merely a more august version of
those other assemblies under sacred trees—the *Bile*—mentioned in the
Irish texts.

All can, therefore, be taken as symbolical centres and the importance
attached to these is shown by the frequency with which the word
"centre" occurs as an element of place names. Examples, are Meath in
Ireland and Medionemeton in Scotland, while even Milan in Italy
comes from Mediolanum.

Although Caesar does not say so in so many words, it was plainly at the
Carnutes' meeting that, when need arose, a new Archdruid was chosen.
He says that, if there were several nominees, an election was held,
"though sometimes," he adds, "they actually fight it out".

Caesar, as we have seen, was anxious to display the Druids as a potent
force in Celtic national unification. Showing them to be an organized
body under its own powerful leadership would, naturally, assist this
cause, and, as he is the only author to mention these facts, the question
of their veracity arises.

Ammianus Marcellinus gives a corroborative hint in his reference to
the Druids' being "bound together in a fraternal organization", but this
is vitiated by the gratuitous information that it had been instituted by
Pythagoras. All the same, it is possible for the first statement to be true
and not the second. In favour of this we have the unity of belief to be
found throughout the Celtic world, with differences of emphasis as the
only major variation. There is, besides, the considerable power the
Druids wielded which transcended the tribal boundaries. Neither of
these could have come about, surely, unless they were united not only in
belief but also administration. It has frequently been argued that the
shaman is, almost by definition, an individualist.

There are, however, several examples, including contemporary ones,
where they have shown themselves capable of organization. One is to be
found among the Shona people of Zimbabwe where, among other things,
entry to their shamanistic priesthood is strictly regulated by an established hierarchy.

But another pointer towards the existence of a central administration is the rigid training programme for novices. Caesar says this could last as long as twenty years, a statement supported by Pomponius Mela (circa AD 43), though as Piggott points out, it may actually have been not twenty but nineteen years, which would have corresponded with the Druidic calendrical cycle.

Pomponius also tells us that much of the training was done in secret caves and remote woods and valleys. There is a plain shamanistic ring to this, but his "much of" is probably significant; in other words not all tuition was carried out in this fashion and for all that oral methods were used it is likely that there was some institutionalized study, as well.

Geoffrey of Monmouth, writing in the 12th Century AD, refers to a "college of two hundred learned men" at Caerleon-on-Usk in Arthur's time, the 6th Century, who were skilled in "astronomy and other arts". If he is reporting anything more substantial than legend, one cannot help wondering whether this is not a late survival of some sort of Druidic training centre, or, at any rate, one associated with the bardic schools which continued down to late times. "Astronomy" would have meant "astrology" and the Irish word for "bards", *filid*, actually means "seers", while the word "bard" itself became virtually synonymous with "Druid".

These bardic colleges continued in Ireland until the 17th Century, and in Scotland into the 18th. All teaching was oral and students were required to memorize what they were taught in a course which lasted anything from seven to twelve years.

At the very least, these lengthy training courses, bringing numbers of student-Druids together, would have provided the nucleus of an organization, which could well have continued after their "graduation".

But organization presupposes leadership which brings us to Caesar's "Archdruid" and his election. As far as his description goes, we can take it he is referring only to the Druids of Gaul as participating in them, since there is no hint anywhere that those of Britain, Ireland or anywhere else travelled to it. Nor, as a matter of fact, is there much evidence that they were organized under any sort of supreme authority within the confines of their own lands. There is, however, a reference to a "chief poet of the Gaels" which would include the Celts of both Ireland and Scotland. In view of the intimate link between poetry and Druidism this could well mean, as Kendrick suggests, that an overall head had once existed.

In almost all the details of its training Druidism is remarkably similar to Brahminism and to the training undergone by the *bramacarin* or novice. Here again, one can detect the shamanistic undertones, for open-air teaching and meditation was also a characteristic of the *bramacarin*'s training.

The notion of rebirth inseparable from the tyro-shaman's quest for enlightenment forms so recurrent a theme in Druidism that one can hardly suppose that this long training period, for a great part of which he would have been cut off from his normal associations, was other than a symbolical process of rebirth. Indeed, in the *Cad Goddeu* (Battle of the Trees), the 6th Century Welsh bard Taliesin, whose work bears markedly Druidic features, speaks of himself as undergoing numerous metamorphoses.

This selfsame notion is expressed in almost the same words by two other Irish poets, Tuan mac Cairill and Amergein, so that presumably these experiences were necessary to becoming a bard.

Much of the training period was, Caesar says, spent in learning verses. Rhyme and alliteration were in origin mnemonic devices so that we can safely conclude they were learning something more than simple poetry. Magic spells, which are actually rituals, usually take the form of rhymes and since the law was passed down by word of mouth one may suppose that, with the Druids as with the Brahmins, it was encapsulated into jingles for easy remembrance.

But in any event, the epic myths would certainly have formed an important part of the corpus of material to be learnt. Bards and Druids must once have been united. "The magical sweet-mouth harpers of Cain Bile" who in *The Cattle Raid of Cooley* come out of the red cataract of Es Ruaid to charm the contending hosts, are, according to the story-teller "Druids of great knowledge". At least two of the classical writers mention Bards, Vates and Druids as enjoying equally high regard in Celtic society. Just as "bards" is related to "seers", so "vates" (or, as it occurs elsewhere, "Ovates") is a rendering of the Irish *fathi* meaning "inspired one". Thus are the three words associated.

In any case, the gift of poetry is, of itself, divine. The Norse Odinn, who has correspondence with two Celtic gods, Lugh and Esus, is, inter alia, God of Poetry, which is the "Precious Mead". One legend tells how he stole it from the evil giant Suttung, from whom he escapes by changing into an eagle (Lugh also changes into an eagle in the Welsh story of *Math Son of Mathonwy*). With it, he flies to Asgard, the home of the gods. In the myth of his own sacrifice to himself by hanging nine days and nights on the World Tree, his rewards include a sup of the "Precious Mead" and the mastery of nine magic songs. Poetry is also the gift he imparts to his favourites such as the mortal hero, Starkad. Through these stories of Odinn, nicknamed "The Great Shaman", we have an indication of the kind of connexion which existed between poetry and shamanism.

Besides, the Celtic bards possessed a quasi-magical power. As

Diodorus tells us, their songs could be of "praise or obloquy". The latter were the *glam dicin* or satires whose victims were normally those who had broken some law, human or divine, though it could even be used for reasons of mere personal caprice or animosity. When King Ailill sends his satirist, Redg, to Cu Chulainn he at once demands the hero's javelin. When this is refused he threatens "to take away Cu Chulainn's good name".

To its intended target this lampooning was, however, more than a mere embarrassment, an archaic version of the sort of attack a public figure might be exposed to from the media today. Face was of quite literally vital importance to the Celts. Like most people given to boasting, reverses could throw them into despair which, as Strabo assures us, reduced them to lethargic, numbed and helpless depression. The entire concept of honour was one which had become institutionalized in Celtic society. Every freeman had his so-called "honour-price" which was the value placed upon his status in the community and included his actual wealth in whatever form it might be expressed. Honour-price could be raised if his fortune or standing increased, but conversely, it could be reduced.

With such a premium on status, it is understandable that the object of a *glam dicin* would feel himself to have suffered an intolerable humiliation. Such indeed were its effects that its shamed victim, rejected by society, could even fall sick and die. It possessed, therefore, the force of a magic spell.

Finally, the Druids, like the shamans, were undoubtedly the "memory of the people" and the form this would have taken was mythology. We have, for example, the obvious recollection of some great, primeval flood in those numerous stories of engulfed cities which continue into Christian times, and are still to be found. There was in fact, a series of natural cataclysms during the 15th Century BC, which included earthquakes, volcanic eruption, tidal waves and hurricanes. The level of the sea rose and great areas of land were flooded (destroying, so some say, the civilization of Atlantis in the process). In any case, these events would account for the proverbial Celtic terror of "the sky falling and the sea bursting its bounds". When Posidonius asked the Druids how the world would end, they told him it would come by fire and water.

With its intermingling of gods and heroes, of worlds of living and dead the mythology represents a species of sacred history, a collection of hierophanies, flattering to its subjects' ego, as is the invariable case, by giving a demonstration of divine regard for them. A precisely similar situation can be found in, for instance, the Hindu myths or, to take a more familiar illustration, the Old Testament. The greater part of this comprises epics with frequent interventions by Yahweh in which he manifests his favour towards his "Chosen People". This being so, one would expect that, as Hindu mythology was entrusted to the guardian-ship of the Brahmins, Celtic mythology would come within the province of its religious leaders.

And the wide distribution of these myths, accompanied by the dis-tribution of the cults of the gods who most frequently figure in them, is in itself further evidence of a basically unified organization to transmit them.

The reward for the successful completion of his studies was, for the graduate Druid, an unrivalled and in many ways unassailable place in Celtic society.

What was the ordinary day-to-day life of the Druid like? If we look at the Brahmins we find that after emerging from the pupil, *bramacarin* stage, they were expected to marry and set up as householders. We know from the frequent references to them in domestic situations that the Druids also married and were householders.

Somewhat more problematic are their sources of income. In the case of the Brahmins, they were prohibited from accepting payment for their services and were requited with "gifts" governed by a strict tariff. Some-thing similar may have obtained among the Druids, especially when they were being employed by individuals, as Caesar indicates could be the case. It is also possible that where they functioned as court-chaplains, they might have been paid some sort of regular income, though the economic dependence it would have involved makes this questionable.

It is, however, conceivable that they may have farmed or even have pursued a trade, such as metal-working, an activity with strongly magi-cal associations.

As to their social standing, all the classical sources are at one in declaring that the Druids were held in the highest esteem. Caesar places them more precisely in the social hierarchy. Only two classes were held of any account in Gaul, he claims: the Druids and the Knights. There is no doubt that the Druids came from the class of *Equites* and may have borne arms, even after entering the order, despite an exemption from military service.

Outside of Gaul a similar situation probably obtained. In Ireland, they are recorded as standing just below the nobility, but we have examples of their being drawn from a higher stratum of society still. Conchobhar, the Ulster chieftain, was the son of the Druid, Cathbadh, who had himself once commanded an army. Since the chieftaincy was restricted to members of a "royal family", this would mean that the Druids might themselves come of royal blood. To a degree, this is confirmed by the example of Diviciacus, the visitor to Rome, who

besides being, on the testimony of Cicero, a Druid, was also chieftain of
the Aedui.

Even in the more numerous cases where a Druid was not of royal
lineage, they are frequently shown as standing in the closest possible
relationship with the king. This goes down to Christian times, though
the Druid has by now become a mere "magician", and it is well exemplified in the Arthur-Merlin duality, for all that Merlin was a latecomer
to the cycle.

Weber speaks of the Brahmins as occupying the position of "court-
chaplains", and one could perhaps use the same phrase of the Druids.
But if it evokes thoughts of those who occupied such positions with the
later, Christian, princes it is misleading. More often, they seem closer to
chancellors and one is reminded of those Renaissance and post-
Renaissance prelates who held such high positions—Richelieu or
Wolsey, for instance. The latter, once reproved by Henry VIII for using
the expression "meus et rex" would have been perfectly safe had he been
a Druid since, as we have seen, the king was not permitted to speak until
his Druid had done so—a nice deference by the temporal to the spiritual.

Their superiority in this respect is not, however, totally surprising
since, at any rate in times of their full power, the king ruled virtually by
permission of the Druids. It was they who were instrumental in his
choosing, as Merlin settles upon Arthur through the test of the sword-
in-the-stone. In Ireland, this was done by means of the *Tarbfeis* or bull-
dream. A bull—that most potent symbol of potency was sacrificed and a
broth prepared from it. The sacrificers then laved in this and ate the
flesh. In a vision which came during the sleep that followed, the identity
of the future king was revealed to them.

The king was also conceived of as the mortal mate of a goddess; their
nuptials, intended to guarantee the prosperity of his reign, being super-
vised by the Druids. In its typical form, the ceremony would take place
at some specially designated well or spring where the king-elect would be
offered a goblet to drink from at the hand of a beautiful girl who personified the goddess and who would duly be sacrificed—the invariable
fate of all mortals upon whom the mantle of divinity fell.

If the description of a ritual practised in the town of Kenelcunnil in
Northern Ulster, recorded by the 13th Century writer Gerald of Wales,
is any guide, it is probable that the couple copulated in public before the
sacrifice. In his *Topographia*, Gerald describes how the new king has
bestial relations with a white mare. This is then sacrificed, its flesh put
into water in which the king bathes. After cooking, the meat is shared
out among the assembly. Since the Celtic pantheon includes an all-
powerful horse-goddess in Epona (Macha in Ireland), it seems safe to
conclude that this ritual represented a late survival of the symbolical
consummation of the marriage of king and deity.

But as a mortal, the king ages, vigour and virility both declining. In sympathy with him, his divine spouse also ages—a state of affairs which woman-like she does not accept with equanimity. The signs that this process is occurring are a succession of poor harvests or other untoward events, showing that the earth has lost its fertility because of the increasing sterility of its patron deity. Only a fresh mate will restore her to youth, beauty and full fecundity.

The king, accordingly, must be sacrificed, and it is probably from this that the various theories of sacrificed kings, which supposedly extend down to the Plantagenets and beyond, get their sanction.[2]

But this end is not one reserved for him solely on account of age, for any train of adversities may be ascribed to the failure of the union and the king dispatched and replaced. The victims were expected to accept their fate philosophically—and usually did. In the *mabinogi* of *Branwen, Daughter of Llyr*, the king, Brân, who is, of course, the god Bran or Brennos, leader of the expeditions against Rome and Delphi, orders his own decapitation after he is wounded in the foot by a poisoned spear. The foot is the customary euphemism for the genitals so that he has actually been rendered impotent, a condition which, for a king, poses a threat to the well-being of his entire people.

Their activities as makers and destroyers of kings gives an illuminating insight into the power and prestige the Druids enjoyed and, quite apart from such material advantages as exemption from tax, makes it understandable why the calling was rarely short of recruits, many as Caesar tells us, "going of their own accord, while others were sent by their parents"—the latter obviously with an eye to a good, progressive career for their offspring.

Throughout the passage describing Druidism, including the references to recruitment and training, Caesar seems to imply it was an entirely masculine foundation. Were there, then, women in it? If we go back to the example of shamanism, we find both sexes to be involved, though with a male predominance. Brahminism, on the other hand, is a wholly male caste.

[2] Such examples of royal sacrifice are to be found in cultures other than the Celtic. When Odinn gave his human favourite, Starkad, the gift of poetry he made clear that he would demand repayment. One morning while Starkad and a group of warriors are with the king, they carry out a mock execution. The gut of a calf is hung on a drooping twig and a noose is set round the neck of the king, who stands on a stump. Starkad strikes him with a reed given to him by Odinn the previous night, saying the word, "Now I give thee to Odinn". At that instant everything changes. The twig becomes a stout branch, the calf's-gut a rope, the reed a spear. The stump topples, the king strangles and Odinn is requited in a fashion highly appropriate as he is himself "God of the Hanged". In another instance, during the reign of King Domaldi of Sweden, first animal then human sacrifice is offered to try to halt the succession of bad harvests which have brought famine. In the end the king decides he must sacrifice himself. When he does the famine ends.

We have, to be sure, Tacitus' black-clad harridans at the Battle of Anglesey and in the two late passages from the *Historia Augusta* Druidesses are mentioned. There is also mention of a woman using the Druidical wand and casting a spell with it in an early Irish tale. But if these were actually Druidesses, it is surprising they were not so described.

Instances of this sort have to be weighed against the far more numerous passages in which the order is presented as expressly male. In no vernacular text is there an explicit reference to Druidesses and only one from which their existence might be inferred. Since one of its characters is a bishop, its late dating may be the explanation of this introduction of a female element. Muirchertach, King of All Ireland, though married, takes in a girl called Sin (the name has no connexion with the Anglo-Saxon word) who turns out to be a witch who brings disaster and the wrath of Mother Church on the *ménage à trois*, ending in the death of Muirchertach.

As Markale points out, the element of feminine sorcery in this is nearer to the later traditions of witchcraft than to Druidism. Much the same can be said of the appearance of "Druidesses" in the *Historia Augusta*. They are indulging in simple prophecy, certainly an activity associated with witches.

The only conclusion to be drawn therefore is that although they might have been associated with Druidism in its latter days, women were never admitted to it in any proper sense.

The only problematical factor is accounting for the various abbesses and anchoresses who make repeated appearances in the Arthurian legends. We know that women played a far more crucial role in the Celtic church than in the later, masculine-dominated Catholic one, but the resemblance between Tacitus' black furies and the black-clad women religious in the Arthurian cycle forces one to consider whether the first were not the true antecedents of the second; the monk-scribes might well have felt this kind of Christianization desirable. While one cannot suppose them to be "Druidesses", they may well have been members of one of the miscellaneous bodies of priestesses, such as those of Cimbri mentioned by Strabo or the ones living on an island who practised the roof-rethatching ritual. The latter are described as being devoted to a "Dionysian" cult, but this probably refers less to the god, Dionysus himself, than to the character of their practices which probably involved frenzy and ecstasy. We may well assume that in all cases, these groups of women were devoted to cults outside the main stream of Celtic religion and Druidism, though probably tolerated by it.

Seen from the point of view of their classical observers, it is understandable that the Druids must have seemed bizarre figures with their wands, their animal-skin costumes and, if our surmise is right, their weird, half-shaven heads and their hair streaming uncut behind them. They must have borne as much resemblance to the dignified *flamens* and *pontifices* as a dancing Dervish bears to a Curia cardinal, and it is comprehensible why they were so studious in avoiding the use of the word "priest" in connexion with them.

And this was to say nothing, of course, of the incredible practices of their religion: the gatherings of worshippers deep in the forest, the festivals celebrated by night rather than day and—most of all—the rendering of human sacrifice.

CHAPTER SEVEN

Lawyers, Doctors, Poets

WHAT would have been no less remarkable to these foreign observers was the penetration of religion into spheres so long secularized in their own societies that their real origins were forgotten.

Outside of their central role as theologians and ministers the Druids were to some extent, as we have already seen, calendarists, seers and mythologues. From the Posidonian sources we know them also to have been their society's jurists. Strabo describes them as "the most just of men", and while this can only be taken as a stereotyped formula rather than a statement of considered opinion, we must put beside it Caesar's description of them as judges, charged among other things, with the investigation of such matters as murder.

Besides criminal cases, they also arbitrated in civil disputes and among the sanctions they could apply was that of banning from attendance at sacrifice those who did not accept their judgments, this bringing in its train social ostracism. Punishments could include, as we know, being consigned to death amid the flames of the burning wicker colossi. We do not know what other punishments were used; possibly flogging and dismemberment. There is no evidence that they had such institutions as prisons and Caesar tells us that death, accompanied by torture, was the lot of those who stole from the piles of war-booty dedicated to the gods. He adds that similar penalties were exacted from the widows of aristocrats whose deaths were thought suspicious. This could well have been a comparatively common occurrence. We know there were "Black Druids", such as Fir Doirch in the story of Sadv and Finn, and this introduces the possibility of black magic and witchcraft killing, like those of which so many unhappy women were unjustly accused and punished in mid-17th Century Britain.

Markale mentions a semi-legal function of the Druids as administrators of oaths, which, he says, the gods were called upon to witness and guarantee. The frequent references to the "sky falling and sea breaking its bounds" derive, he suggests, from this. In other words a typical oath might run "If I fail to observe my pledges may the sky fall and destroy me, and the sea overflow and drown me".

On the quality of Druidic jurisprudence it is difficult to pronounce. It was, no doubt, as Kendrick says, "a fairly well-defined code enforcing the sanctity of human life and of personal and public property." Disputes requiring their judicial arbitration must have been relatively common. Boundary disputes involving both clans and tribes would have needed resolution and the incessant tribal warfare would have called for considerable negotiating skill when it came to drawing up peace treaties. We can also envisage that customs such as cliency would have been fraught with legal pitfalls needing much forensic skill for their resolution.

On the other hand, the survival of clan and family feuding late into Celtic history suggests that there must have been gaps in the administration of justice compelling those with grievances to take matters into their own hands. Nor can one ignore Caesar's comment that while the victims of the Druidic holocausts were in the main convicted criminals, they did not hesitate to make up numbers with innocent people, if this was necessary. This seems to accord with a peculiarly Druidic concept of Cosmic balance.

In any event an enormous body of law must have been involved, making it all the more amazing that it was wholly oral.

From Caesar we learn that another function of the Druids was that of acting as teachers, a statement confirmed not only by Pomponius Mela, but also from the Irish texts. In *The Cattle Raid of Cooley*, the Druid, Cathbadh, is mentioned as "imparting learning to his pupils" and we have them also as instructors of the women of the royal houses. Even the warrior-hero, Cu Chulainn, is supposed to have been the pupil of a Druid. The actual content of their teaching can only be a matter for conjecture. Kendrick, who regards their control of education as one of the Druids' principal weapons in maintaining power, intimates that it consisted mainly of *Druidecht*, the lore of Druidism, which in practical terms could have meant little more than teaching based on the myths, since the close secrets of the order most certainly were never divulged to the laity. But it is also possible that it included what we should now call "basic literacy and numeracy". The Celts used the Greek alphabet, for writing as we know not only from Caesar, but also from inscriptions such as those on coinage. They also seemed to have taken some pains to render the phonetic values of their language accurately, as for example, by adding a bar through the letters D and S to indicate sounds which did not exist in Greek. This implies that there were enough people who could make out such symbols to justify the effort involved. Furthermore, according to Caesar one reason for the Druids' refusal to commit their teachings to writing was to keep them secret; this precaution would have been unnecessary if they were the only people who could read or write.

Besides being its lawyers and teachers, they were also their community's physicians. The "holy healers" summoned to attend King Conchobhar after a sling shot had lodged in his forehead must, surely, have been Druids, while Tiberius' edict banning Druidism to Roman citizens specifically mentions them as 'the whole tribe of prophets and physicians'.

The basis of their skill was, of course, herbalism. In *The Natural History*, Pliny is primarily concerned to describe the medicinal properties of herbs which, in the case of mistletoe, he says the Celts called by a word meaning "all healing". This practical application of it appears at variance with the ideas of other cultures, such as Norse which valued the plant solely on account of its supposed divine origins.

In point of fact, even to us the concepts involved here are less unfamiliar than they might appear to be at first glance. The laws of a society are always deeply rooted in its religious beliefs. The tablets of stone bearing the Ten Commandments, to cite the best known example, were entrusted by God himself to Moses, who in his turn serves as their interpreter and is succeeded by a whole line of Jewish religious jurists.

The care of the sick was originally carried out by religious bodies as the word "hospital" indicates and to a greater or lesser extent this tradition continues, as do schools under religious patronage. The monasteries were also the centres of astronomical observation. As early as the Anglo-Saxon Chronicle notes on such events as eclipses are given, while Copernicus, "the father of modern astronomy", operated under direct ecclesiastical patronage as a lay canon of Frauenberg Cathedral. The modern calendar even bears the name of Pope Gregory XIII who introduced it.

In any case, both calendar-making and the astronomical observation necessary for it would have been essential to the correct execution of ritual. The state of the moon would have to be known, as in the case of the mistletoe-gathering ceremony which Pliny says took place on the sixth day of the new moon, or in deciding the proper day for the celebration of a festival. This would have been a particular problem for the Druids, since the system they used to synchronize solar and lunar time involved the introduction of intercalary months of thirty days at intervals of two-and-a-half and three years in alternation (as opposed to our own system of inserting an extra day every four years). One has to suppose, therefore, that celebration of festivals was determined by the positions of sun or moon rather than by assigning fixed days each year to them. A similarity is to be found in the 'Golden Number' used to calculate the moveable feast of Easter in Christianity, and this was also formerly used for calculating Christmas. Significantly enough, the Golden Number is itself based on lunar reckoning and on the nineteen-year Metonic cycle employed by the Druids. Druidic herbalism obviously extended to what we should now call veterinary practice. Not only does this lie very much within the province of the shaman, but Pliny tells us explicitly that among the virtues of mistletoe was that of giving fertility to barren animals.

One would, however, be wrong I think to suppose that Druidic skill limited itself to those activities we associate with simple rural life, for it may well have gone much further.

Though it was basically an agrarian society, the Celtic was at least nascently a technological and, above all, an heroic one and as such preoccupied not only with its warrior-heroes, but also with weaponry. Spears and swords make frequent appearance in legend and are found in votive deposits. The *Cattle Raid* provides a page-long list of them and the various heroes who had wielded them. They included Lamthapad, the sword of Conall Cernach whom Ross tentatively equates with Cernunnos. Nuada's sword was one of the most treasured possessions of that great family of gods called the *Tuatha De Danann*, the People of Dana. Lugh's spear, which also belonged to the *tuatha*, was of such a nature that 'the woman or man who held it could not be conquered in battle'. It was of a potency which made it necessary to keep it immersed in a cauldron of water when not in use or the town in which it was housed would have been burnt down. The spear mentioned in the Grail legend had similar properties: its merest scratch could be fatal. If the thrower uttered the magic word *"ibar"* as it left his hand, it never missed its mark; if he said *"athibar"*, it came back to him. Arthur's right to the throne was determined by the drawing of the sword from the stone and he later received the magical Excalibur through Merlin. In an extant Manx legend, Manannan mac Lir, the island's divine founder, possesses not only a swift horse, Enbarr, but also a death-dealing sword The Answerer.

All this emphasis on magical weapons suggests a connexion with the Druids, that, in other words, they were their suppliers—as Merlin supplied Arthur with Excalibur—an activity which may, indeed, have provided a source of income for them. This posits a knowledge of metallurgy and practical metal-working on their part and it seems to me extremely likely they possessed both.

It is not only agriculture and husbandry which mythology ascribes to divine founders: technology, too, comes from this source. For this reason, smith-gods are to be found in many metal-using cultures. With the Celts it was Goibniu, the Welsh Govannon, son of Don or Dana, and hence one of the *Tuatha De Danann*. In Irish poetry he is celebrated as the maker of sharp weapons. As we know from the practices of alchemy, the working of metals is closely allied with magic, the alchemists' seven metals corresponding with the seven planets which were supposed to exert their influence upon them.

We have analogies in many heroic societies; among them was that of the Zulus of South Africa. Shaka, their great king, had his spear specially wrought in a foundry, run under the auspices of witch-doctors, which lay in the forest.

Supernatural foundries in the depths of forests or mountain hideouts, are the very stuff of myth, and the small scale of operation implied is perfectly possible. Even in Roman times many foundries employed no more than two or three people. In parts of the Middle East today it is possible to see individual craftsmen working, sometimes with one assistant, sometimes alone, in their backstreet premises.

Moreover, during the manufacturing process one step in particular lends itself to quasi-magical practice. This is tempering, the crucial point at which the blade is given the surface hardness which allows it to take and hold its cutting edge. This involves heating the blade to the correct temperature, then plunging it in a liquid. Usually this is oil or water, depending on the type of surface required, but some smiths, especially those in the Middle East, preferred to use blood because it yields phosphorus.

As both Arabs and Celts are likely to have derived their knowledge of iron-working from the same source, it is probable that they also used blood. This would bring in somthing akin to sacrifice and hence involve the invocation of a deity. In a real sense, therefore, these would be magic weapons.

There is actual evidence that the Celts had two qualities of blade. Celtic swords were highly sought after, as were the Arab ones later. Certainly, those which have survived to come down to us and which would, one supposes, have belonged to the wealthier members of society, are of admirable quality. On the other hand, Polybius in his description of the Battle of Telamon speaks of blades so poor they required straightening after every blow. These presumably would have been the blades belonging to the majority of men, who could not afford the "magical" Druidic blades.

Since it was one of the undoubted foundations of their power, it was naturally in the Druids' interest to present their activities as magical. But this was certainly no deliberate contrivance, for in many cases the results of their activities would have been as unaccountable to themselves as to observers. Most typical of these would have been things like water-divining and hypnotism, for whose employment by the Druids we have at least circumstantial evidence.

The discovery of water-sources would have been of vital importance to migratory peoples. The willow and hazel, the two trees whose wood is most favoured by dowsers for their divining rods, were among those most venerated by Druidism and one must not forget that the traditional wand may well have had its origins in practice of this sort. Water-divining techniques are also sometimes used in the detection of metallic ore and this, too, would have been of importance to the Celts who used bronze and later iron. This brings in the whole question of "radiesthesia" about which so much passionate argument rages.[1] Whether or not its scientific base is sound, it seems likely that the Druids would have used something of the sort. In any case, a passage in one of the stories of Cu Chulainn is not uninstructive in this connexion. Awakened by noise outside, the hero rushes out. He sees an old woman in a chariot, drawn by a horse with a single leg, the animal apparently being held upright by the chariot-pole which goes right through its body to be held in place by a peg where the end of the pole emerges from its forehead. The whole image is reminiscent of the waggon- and chariot-burials of the Scythians, in which a chieftain was laid out in a chariot, drawn by his favourite horse. This was slain and stuffed for the purpose and held upright by a pole driven through the entire length of the body and also secured by a peg at the head.

In the scene witnessed by Cu Chulainn the association with death is emphasized by the fact that the horse, the woman and the cloak she wears are all red, the Other World colour. But what gives the story its special relevance is that a man, who is walking beside the chariot, holds in his hand a fork of hazel—in other words, the precise instrument of the

[1] Recent researches, whose results are still tentative and debatable, suggest a possible connexion between methods used in water-divining and the earth's magnetic-field. This in its turn introduces the whole, highly contentious topic of the so-called Ley Lines which are supposedly lines of magnetic-force. Some advocates of the theory claim that not only Stonehenge, but other henges and stone-circles stand at the junction points of Ley Lines and that a kind of dowsing technique was used for the determination of where the buildings should be sited as well as for other purposes connected with their use as astronomical computers.

water-diviner. The couple give the impression of being lost, and when one remembers that the Other World could be entered by way of the waters, the hazel fork carried by the man is surely explained.

It is Cu Chulainn, too, who gives us our most explicit glimpse of hypnotism. He was himself the pupil of a Druid and it is plain that Cathbadh vouchsafed him much more than his class-mates. When, one day, the hero's chariot is halted by a recalcitrant herd of deer, he simply descends and hypnotises both the deer and his own startled horses. "I swear by the god of the Ulstermen," he tells them, "that because of the look I shall give them, the horses shall not depart from their true path, and because of the look I shall give the deer, they will bow their heads in awe of me and not move."

The "magic sleep" attributed to the Druids must also have been hypnotic trance and one suspects something analogous in those strange, soporific songs such as that sung by Angus and his love when, in swan form, they fly thrice round the lake. It may well lie behind that gift of shape-shifting, possessed by the gods, but shared by Druids in so many stories about them.

But there are, in any case, two passages in the classical sources which read like demonstrations of hypnosis. One comes from Tacitus' account of the Battle of Anglesey. Here the Druids are graphically described calling down divine wrath with hands uplifted to heaven—a gesture of invocation copied by the Celtic Christians and still retained in some fundamentalist sects, notably in Northern Ireland. The scene recalls the description of Druidic intervention in inter-tribal warfare where, as Strabo and Diodorus record, they were able to make the contenders "stop when they were about to line up for battle". On closer examination, the similarity becomes even more striking. Diodorus tells us, "Often when the combatants are ranged face to face, the swords are drawn and spears bristling, these men come between the armies and stay the battle, just as wild animals are sometimes held spellbound". This compares intriguingly with Tacitus's account of the effect of the Druids' presence on the shores of Anglesey. The seasoned Roman troops were so awestruck "that, as if their limbs were paralysed, they stood motionless and exposed to wounds". This spell could be broken only by the generals themselves, who would, presumably, have been in the rear and so unaffected.

The mass-hypnosis which is implied in these latter instances is, however, an occurrence of such rarity that many authorities question its validity, pointing out that by no means everyone is susceptible to hypnosis anyway. But perhaps we should not forget those examples of mass-hypnosis known to our own times in such phenomena as the Nuremberg Rallies or, for that matter, in contemporary pop festivals.

And account should also be taken of the increased suggestibility of peoples in certain cultural or social circumstances. It is this which must explain the success of the ritual cursing of African witch-doctors. There is a wealth of evidence to show that this could lead to the actual death of its victim. Under British rule, African witch-doctors who employed such methods could be hanged as murderers and in some emergent African states the casting of fatal spells is still a capital crime.

The potency of Druidic malediction as demonstrated in the case of the attack on Anglesey would also lend force to what were in the final analysis other techniques of spell-binding: the *glam dicin*, which we have already discussed and the *geas*. The *geas* was a form of taboo whereby the individual upon whom it was laid was threatened with the immediate invocation of a malign fate if he performed a particular act or series of acts. These results were not merely unpleasant and normally fatal, they were also shameful and the *geas* could be used not merely as a prohibition, but equally as a means of compelling an individual to adopt a particular course of action. Forcing him to break his *geas* was one way in which a hero could be destroyed and in the stories of Cu Chulainn, the hero who is prohibited from eating dog-meat (his nickname "Cu" actually means "dog"), is constantly assailed by enemies trying to make him do so. When, inadvertently, he does the result is fatal.

The inevitability with which *geasa* will be broken is one of the constant elements of many of the stories and is one which introduces an almost Greek fatalism into Celtic thought.

Markale implies that the practical application of the *geas* was as a means of making contracts binding, but, while it may have been applied to this, it had, I think, deeper origins associated with prophecy. The most characteristic case is the famous *geas* laid on Derdriu, or "Deirdre of the Sorrows", as she is most commonly called. As an unborn babe she screams with such force that the men rush for their weapons. The Druid, Cathbadh, with her mother before him expatiates on the extraordinary beauty the child will possess. Then he predicts that she will bring evil— torments to Ulster, jealousy, quarrelling and the death of great heroes, "little graves everywhere", as he puts it.

He cannot be accused of cursing the girl or of laying a spell on her, he is simply predicting the future and his prognostications come to be fully justified.

What, however, is to be made of this whole broad subject of Druidic divination?

Strabo and Diodorus present the practice of taking auspices from the blood-flow and death struggles of a stabbed man as something uniquely Celtic. In fact, it was known in many societies. The Romans actually had a word for it—*haruspicy*, from the Etruscan *haruspex*, the name given to the priests specializing in it. It may well have been from the Etruscans that the Druids took it. Although by republican times the Romans no longer practised human sacrifice, they had earlier, and haruspicy probably simply transferred itself from human to animal victim.

Of many of the methods of divination, one is compelled to agree with Kendrick that they need not be taken too seriously. The wheel of the Irish Druids was probably little more than an early version of those devices known to Victorian parlour entertainments in which an arrow was spun over a disk to stop at some phrase like "A fair stranger awaits your love". The *imbas forasnai* mentioned in the *Cattle Raid*, though not necessarily Druidic, may have been a form of palm-reading, though other translations are possible.

Prophecy by the movements of clouds has about it the ring of folk-meteorology and one may well suppose that this was the sort of thing the Druids would have practised. There is also, of course, the possibility of a connexion with rain-making, another practice which on the analogy of shamanism we might justifiably associate with them. One of their most important deities, Nuada or Nodens, is surnamed the "Cloud-Maker" and could well have been invoked no doubt with human sacrifice at times of drought. What one wonders is whether there is not a close link between the shamanic practice of rain-making and the whole evolution of the idea of deities. Spirits able to control the elements would have been ones of formidable power evoking special respect.

Prediction from the flight of birds may have originated in the period of Celtic migrations, when observations of the kind of birdlife would have been a helpful guide to the knowledgeable about the characteristics of the terrain they were approaching. A simple ecological fact is involved: birds would be found in their greatest numbers where food was most abundant.

Belief in this form of divination was, however, obviously deeply ground for as late as Geoffrey of Monmouth instances of it are to be found. He relates how, in the time of Arthur, eagles were said to flock together on the islands of Loch Lomond. emitting a shrill scream by which it was possible to foretell "any prodigious event which was about to occur in the kingdom".

The interpretation of birds' cries would plainly come within the province of the Druids, who were believed to understand bird-language—a notably shamanistic gift. Thanks to it, they were able to use species besides the eagle. The raven, for example, prophesied by both its cry and its flight, often, as might be anticipated, presaging doom. This bird occurs so frequently in myth and has so repeatedly been found, represented in all sorts of materials in votive deposits, that one suspects a totemic origin. The name Brân means raven, for example. The Mórrígan often appears as a raven and in one context Macha, too, is so glossed.

The Irish Badb also appears as a battle-raven and in one of the Welsh stories Arthur's troops are accused of attacking Owein's ravens, but here what seems to be meant is another army, which would link them with the various raven-goddesses who appear, like the Badb, in time of war. There are, in fact, two characteristics of the bird which would connect it with war and warriors. The first is the extreme courage of the males, who in protecting their young will drive off the attacks of bigger birds like the kite, and even in many cases, of cats. The second is that as a carrion-bird its appearance on battlefields is well known. It is said to foretell battle, so that it is often taken by soldiers on the march as an indication that an engagement will soon be fought.

Strangely enough, the pert and innocent-looking wren is also regarded as a bird of ill-omen, warning, among other things, of the deaths of great men. Killip suggests that the wren was taken for a transformed enchantress who, in typically Celtic fashion, lured men to their deaths beneath the waters. Certainly, as we have already seen, with the raven and the eagle, birds were repeatedly equated with the Other World and were plainly regarded as being able freely to cross the boundaries dividing the two planes of existence, reason enough for Other World beings to assume their guise.

The prophetic gifts of the Druids did not, of course, express themselves only through the interpretation of signs. They were prophets in their own right. The two examples of "Druidesses" making predictions which later came true, quoted from the *Historia Augusta* in Chapter Four, are the kind of colourful, "human interest" material more appropriate to the popular press than history books, but in one episode in the *Cattle Raid*, the Druid, Cathbadh, is asked by one of his pupils to prophesy on the spur of the moment. He answers, "The little boy who takes up arms this day shall be splendid and renowned for his deeds". The boy so designated is, of course, Cu Chulainn.

What we are here confronted by is "Second Sight" or just "The Sight", that supernatural gift found particularly among the Irish and the Highlanders of Scotland and manifesting itself in its most potent form in the seventh son of a seventh son. It is a gift in the most real of senses that it is granted only to the few, upon whom, as Professor Ross says in her book *Folklore of the Highlands*, it often weighed heavily. As one might expect, it is not always pleasant to know what the future holds for oneself or for others.

Strabo and Diodorus, as we know, specifically mention *vates* or seers as among the three kinds of men enjoying highest esteem in Celtic life. There is some reason for supposing that bards could be regarded as more or less a sub-division of Druidism, though one which gathered more and more independence with the passage of time. The seers, on the other hand, must have occupied an independent position from the outset, since there was no way a man could become one save by having been endowed with the gift of "The Sight". This does not, of course, mean they were regarded other than as Druids; they were, no doubt, a branch of the order.

One may well suspect that there would have been other divisions, for however sceptical one might be about the actual content of Druidic knowledge, it is scarcely possible to deny its magnitude which would have made division and specialization essential. Whether training took nineteen or twenty years, Caesar and Pomponious can hardly have been exaggerating and it is not surprising that so many classical writers saw the order in general as a vast repository of knowledge. This, of course, reached its most preposterous lengths among the later and more idealizing descriptions by those who, imbued with the Platonic tradition, were quick to seize on the now largely defunct Druids as examples of the "philosopher-kings" of the Utopian *Republic*.

Without making concessions to these more extravagant claims, one might still reconsider the actual character of Druidic knowledge in the light of their association with bodies like the Brahmins and the Magi.

The first thing to come to mind is their supposed link with Pythagoras. Hitherto, this has been thought to rest wholly on the shared belief in the transmigration of the soul. But there are, in fact, other parallels. Pythagoras' interest in music is demonstrated by his discovery of the musical interval—that is to say, the relation between the length of string and the frequency of the note it produces. Celtic society was one in which music was highly valued (as it still is). Skill in its performance is frequently referred to in the myths; it was certainly used in ritual, while the bardic epics were originally intended to be sung to the reciter's own accompaniment. Bardship was, as we know, closely allied to Druidism. Even in Greek myth, the lyre, developed by the Celts into the harp, is said to have been revealed to mankind by two deities closely associated with magic and shamamism, Apollo and Hermes. Pythagoras, in his turn, is linked with Apollo. Nor was he a mere devotee of his cult: in one text, he is actually described as being the son of the god!

But Pythagoras is also and primarily a mathematician so passionate about his discipline that he was convinced that numerical relationships lay at the heart of the entire universe. This view was also held by the Babylonian priests and to some degree by the Brahmins and possibly the Magi. We cannot be certain about the Druids though they also possessed considerable mathematical knowledge. As their astronomy expressed itself in astrology, so their mathematical knowledge would have been expressed—like that of Babylonian priests, Magi and Brahmins—as numerology, the magic of numbers and their interrelationships. Numbers are certainly pregnant with mystery. There is, for example, the paradox of zero (said to have been discovered by the Brahmins) and the minus quantity; the contradictory characteristics of unity, both indivisible and divisible; or the staggering qualities of infinity. Or there is the strange behaviour of the square of three, itself a holy number to the Druids.[2] But numerology was something in which Pythagoras was himself profoundly interested.

This brings us to an even more surprising, if highly contentious point. Many of the stone circles are not circles at all, but egg-shaped ellipses, ovals wider at one end than the other. One way of producing such a shape is by means of two circles, a smaller and a greater, drawn in such a way that the smaller circle's circumference overlaps that of the greater. The two are then connected to each other by means of tangential lines. And this, according to B R Hallam, is what the Neolithic designers of the megaliths did. The objection is that this method does not produce a true ovoid; it produces one with two straight sides, whereas aerial photographs show the ellipses in question to consist of continuous curves. Professor A Thom has shown that one way of solving the problem is to base the design on calculations using the right-angled or Pythagorean triangle. The implication is that the most famous of his ideas, Pythagoras actually derived from shamanic sources.

And here one is reminded of all the legends connecting Pythagoras with various such sources, including the Druids. One of the earliest of these, and hence that nearest to his own lifetime, comes from Hecateus, for whom Pythagoras' instructor is supposed to have been a certain Abaris, who seems to have been taken for a British Druid, or at least, a shaman practising in Britain.

As an admonition to caution, one need only say that one is here in the realm of those legends which unfailingly attach themselves to the names of famous men and that Pythagoras himself hardly assisted the disentangling of fact from fantasy by omitting to leave any written account of his work behind him.[3]

There are, nonetheless, three indisputable facts: one, that most writers connect Pythagoras with a mysterious cult of shamanistic character; two, that among the descendants of what I have called 'the supershamans', namely the Babylonic priests, the Brahmins and the Magi,

[2] Nine is the number into which, during mathematical operations, other numbers most often tend to resolve themselves. For example, take any three (or more) digits (say 345). Reverse their order (543). Take the lesser from the greater (543-345=198). Add the digits together (1+9+8=18). Add them together again (1+8=9).

[3] Even his association with the Euclidean Proposition, which has made him so hated by generations of schoolchildren, is apocryphal, for all that he was said to have sacrificed a hecatomb (a thousand oxen) in honour of the discovery that the square on the hypotenuse equalled the sum of the squares on the other two sides.

were outstanding mathematicians, like Pythagoras himself; three, that they held a number of beliefs, of which transmigration was one, in common. It could conceivably be argued that, in these circumstances, his failure to commit his work and observations to writing was precisely because those with whom he had been in contact had sworn him to secrecy. As we know, the Druids were unshakable in their determination not to put their doctrines into writing and so, for centuries, were the Brahmins.[4]

[4] The fact that writers are so confused as to who his instructor was, that Pythagoras is variously associated with Druids, Brahmins and the Babylonians (or, as the text says, Assyrians), shows how similar all three must have appeared to the Greek mind.

CHAPTER EIGHT

The Mysterious Gods

WHILE it is easy to understand the astonishment which seized the classical writers at the involvement of what they regarded as ministers of religion in such a multiplicity of functions, it is also easy to understand how it came about.

Societies like the Celtic, believing that they alone occupied the Great Cosmic Centre, the very point at which the numen reached out to make its contact with humanity, were convinced that it was their acts, more than anyone else's, which sustained life and kept the world on its axis. As Soustelle points out in describing the centrality of religious observance to Aztec life, it is only by rituals faithfully and meticulously carried out that cataclysm is averted and chaos kept at bay. Thus religion was by no means the extra duty, the hedging of one's bets with Providence, it had become for the Romans or was to become for Christians even in the so-called "Ages of Faith". This is why the Gauls appeared as incorrigibly superstitious to foreign observers of them.

The matrix of belief was their mythology. It was through this that men learnt that, as nothing happened without cause in their day-to-day existence, causative agencies were to be found in the Cosmos itself. The acts of the gods or their deliberate decisions were responsible for the genesis of the race, and through it of mankind; for the great crises of flood, earthquake and plague, even for such repetitive occurrences as the succession of the seasons or the rising of the sun in the morning. And merely to take these sequences for granted was a perilous act of *hubris*. The empirical facts of bad harvests, drought or disease among the livestock were there to prove that the gods were not mocked.

Between men and their gods, as myth described them, stood the Druids, at once mediators and interpreters, because they stood in a relationship with the gods so intimate it was as though they themselves partook of the divine character.

And for their part, too, the gods are magicians of an unassailable potency who in the use of their powers must be alternatively restrained or encouraged.

As this magical character provides something of the key to our understanding of them, so it also poses riddles of its own. Indeed, this entire area of Celtic deities is one fraught with queries. Caesar lists six "principal" gods to the Gauls: Dispater (or Pluto), Mercury, Mars, Apollo, Jupiter and Minerva. He makes no claim to comprehensiveness, but even if we add to his list the names of those Celtic gods who, from their incidence in place-names, epigraphy and mythology, we can be sure were worshipped over a wide area, we are still left far short of the 374 god-names made out by scholars of which no fewer than 305 occur only once.

That we are not dealing with an equal number of distinct deities is certain, if for no other reason because of the Celtic practice of using different names in different localities. The father-god *In Dagda* becomes *In Ruad Rofhessa*, "the Red One of Great Wisdom" in some places; *Eochaid Ollathair* in others. The last form introduces a *horse*-element, *eoch*- into the name which might well lead the unwary to conclude that here was a totally different being.

There were, too, the numerous territorial divinities, associated with specific geographical features, like Deva, goddess of the River Dee, or Clota, goddess of the Clyde. There are the many important European rivers whose names can be traced back to Celtic gods.

Then there were those which must have been purely tribal gods, whose existence can be inferred from the very nature of Celtic society and its constant internecine wars, but which is supported by the god-names found only in one area.

The necessary adjustments made, we are left, all the same, with a formidable total. How many could, with accuracy, be identified with the Druids? All, says Kendrick, and though one might agree in the sense that the Druids' objective was to dominate Celtic religion in all its facets, some clarification is needed. Somehow we must try to separate the strands of the tangled skein of this huge pantheon, and to do so have to go back as far as we can to the origins of their gods and, indeed, to the roots of the idea of deities itself.

The habitat of the shaman is, as we have seen, within the heart of nature and its forces. In trance, his guides are the spirits of those animals familiar to him either from observation or from the hunt. Indeed, the shaman's role comes into existence because of the need the hunter feels to "make peace" with the spirits of the creatures he kills. But in this world of ghostly-animals, as in that of living ones, it is the most potent animals who occupy the dominant positions: the fierce, courageous boar; the powerful and virile bull; the fleet reindeer; the bear; the horse; the eagle; perhaps the raven; the salmon. All are to be found in the Celtic supernatural, just as we find animal-headed gods among the Egyptians and the Hindus.

And in the ecology of the Other World, too, the lesser creatures play their subordinate roles: for example, the egret perches on the bull's back to cleanse it of vermin, as it is to be seen represented on a carved stone found in Paris in 1711.

Between the shaman and his "guides" special relationships would come to be forged: a "bull spirit", a "bear spirit" or an "eagle spirit" would become friend and benefactor. Dressing himself in the creature's likeness, that he might be recognizable, it would be this "spirit friend" that the shaman would seek out on his own travels through the Other World. The "guide" would show his own goodwill towards the living in a host of ways.

Hunters know of and often form special relationships with a single animal in a hunted species—usually a female—which will actually assist them in their task. It will act, quite voluntarily, as a decoy attracting other members of the herd to where the hunter lies in wait. Those of early times would probably have regarded such animals as supernatural allies and they may well offer a clue to the interpretation of legends about creatures like the "supernatural" boar, Twrc Trywth, or the mysterious white hart which appears in the Arthurian and other stories.

There are also, of course, the numerous stories of birds' becoming emissaries to lead the way to new pastures. Titus Livy (59 BC—AD 17) relates how Ambiganus, king of the Bituriges, among the most powerful of the Gaulish tribes (their name means, according to Markale, "Kings of the Earth"), growing old and believing his realm to be too big, instructed his nephews, Bellovesus and Sigoevsus, to seek out new lands for at least part of his people. They were to take with them such numbers as would make their progress and final settlement irresistible and their quest would be guided by the will of the gods, as manifested by the flight of birds. One can well envisage from the frequency with which avian couriers occur in Celtic myth that what Livy described was a well-established tradition.

For such favours as the shaman's guide displayed towards them, the tribe would want not only to show its gratitude, but also to ensure their continuance. Among other ways of honouring him would be by representations set up in prominent places where all might see and be reminded. The tribe might also take his name and display his likeness on its battle shields. He has become, we should say, a totem.

The road that leads from here to full deification may be long, but its final destination is inevitable. May it not be that the creature that bestows one favour bestows all? It calls for little discernment to see how close the Celts were to this totemic feeling. Lugh takes on the likeness of an eagle in one myth, that of a salmon in another. Angus, son of In Dagda, is himself sometimes given a horse-name and takes on the form of a swan.

But there are besides the wider questions, those for example of the origins of the tribes, of humanity, of life itself. May it not be that these, too, derive from some beneficent animal? To find communities tracing their ancestry back to a totemic animal is, of course, common enough.

There is the wolf which suckled Romulus and Remus, twin founders of Rome. The Scythian tribes traced their lineage in the same way. There are numerous Celtic mother-goddesses who are associated with animals: the cow; the pig; the bear. It may well be that the Arduinna, associated with the boar or Mathonwy, mother of Math, whose name associates her with the bear (Matu), were in origin tribal mother-deities who, in the course of time passed into a general, as it were racial, mythology.

But for the Celts, pride of place among these totemic creatures must surely be accorded to the horse. As one of the first great horse-using peoples, they had probably been introduced to it as beast of burden by the Scythians, though both races may well have hunted and eaten it or even grazed it and drunk mare's milk for centuries before they put it to other employment. The Indo-European word, *Ekuos*, is the base of the word for "horse" used in most languages, including the Greek *hippos* and the Latin *equus*, both probably derived from the Celtic. So one finds standing high among the *deae matres* of the Celts, the Gaulish Epona, "the Great Horse". Under her Welsh form of Rhiannon, she bears a child abducted at birth. As punishment she has to carry guests to the court of her husband, Pwyll, upon her back. Their offspring, meanwhile, is found outside the stable of a mare which has just foaled. The pregnant Macha, the Irish "Great Horse", curses the Ulstermen when they insist she takes part in a horse-race just before she is due to be delivered. As her chariot reaches the end of the field, she gives birth to twins, a boy and girl; as a consequence the place is called Emain Macha, "Twins of Macha" thereafter. In these stories one catches the hint of some early foundation myth in which the race and perhaps all living things sprang from the belly of a great, totemic mare.

Totems are a long way from the concept of gods, however, and Georges Dumezil in *Les Dieux des Indo-Européens* has pointed to the existence among the Indo-Europeans of a word, *deiwos*, used to describe creatures in the likeness of humans, but possessing superhuman powers. This is plainly the radical of most of the words for "god" in the European tongues: the Greek *theos*, the Latin *deo*, the Spanish, *dios*, the French *dieu*, for example.

As the title of his book implies, he goes further than this and claims to distinguish a group of deities common to all the Indo-European races. There are, thus, the gods of wealth and fertility; the divine warriors: Indra of the Hindus; Mars of the Romans; Thor of the Scandinavians. There are the gods of law and justice: Mitra; the Greek Zeus; Fides; Tyr. But standing in opposition to Mitra is Varuna; to Zeus, Uranus; to Fides, Jupiter; and to Tyr, Odinn (similar juxtapositions are also to be found in Persian religion and, as a matter of fact, in Babylonian). Varuna, Uranus, Jupiter, Odinn, are all designated by Dumezil as "the great, furious magical kings".

While not all scholars would agree wih Dumezil's more far-reaching conclusions, most would unhesitatingly subscribe to the view that there are such marked similarities between many of the gods found among the Indo-European peoples as would postulate a common origin. It is for this reason that Caesar is able to render his six Gaulish gods in terms of their Graeco-Roman counterparts.

Dumezil's "magical kings" provide us I think, with a valuable key to the Celtic pantheon. As we know, only one mortal is qualified to enter the world of the spirits—the shaman—and the "magical kings", almost by definition, all have shamanic links. Odinn is actually nicknamed "the Great Shaman". By his sacrifice, he recapitulates the initiation, symbolical death and regeneration of the shaman. Even his reward takes the form of magical skill. What we have in Odinn, therefore, is a shaman joined with the world of spirits. If we admit to the degree of gods only beings in human likeness, it is surely the "shaman-become-god" who is its founder-member.

And if we can detect him among the Celtic gods we have, surely, one thread we can disentangle. Let us return to Caesar's six, which may well have come from Posidonius. The chief of these was, he says, Jupiter, though the one most venerated was Mercury, represented in countless images and regarded as inventor of the arts, director of travellers and as a powerful supporter of trade and commerce. Dispater was regarded as the common ancestor of the Gauls and it was on account of this that they measured time by nights rather than days and fixed the dates of festivals by the night.

When one tries to turn the list back into its Celtic originals, however, one is quickly led into the realm of conjecture. Jupiter must be Taranis.

Apollo is, almost certainly, Belenos. Dispater is likely to be the horned-god Cernunnos.

With Mercury on the other hand we are faced by a choice: the obvious one is Lugh the Many Skilled, but on a stone discovered at Trèves in 1895 Esus is linked with Mercury. The problem is further confused by the Berne *scholiasts* who equate Esus with Mars, though the answer here is that they probably mean Mars not as war-god but as god of pastoral-ism and Esus certainly had his pastoral character. The god most often rendered as Mars is, in fact, Teutatis, and on the Gundestrup Caul-dron he is certainly shown in association with warriors.

Minerva, the only one remaining, is sheer speculation and I can only hazard Epona, the horse-goddess.

My own form of Caesar's list would be, therefore: Taranis, Belenos, Cernunnos, Esus, Teutatis and ?Epona. And what we have is, undoubt-edly, a group of six extremely powerful Celtic gods. Taranis is repre-sented in numerous dedications. He is the god associated with the oak-tree and hence with Druidism, a link made explicit by Pliny's description of the mistletoe-culling rite. He is, obviously, the god represented on the so-called "Jupiter-columns" found in north eastern and central Gaul where, often, he is portrayed holding a thunder bolt, like Jupiter, or a wheel, his other attribute. It is surely his name which is commemorated in the name of the isle of Taransay in Harris and in the chapel of Saint Tarran which stands on it.

The name Belenos occurs on thirty-two dedications and he was invoked over an area which runs from Northern Italy—the old Cisalpine Gaul—to the Shetlands. Cymbeline, the historical king on whom Shakespeare based his play is, correctly, Cuno-Belenos, the "Hound of Belenos". As we saw earlier, he is still associated, at least in name, with May Day festivals in many parts of the Celtic world.

For the Celtic Mercury I have settled on Esus in preference to Lugh because the latter comes from a totally different strain of deities, as I shall demonstrate shortly.

If we regard Esus as Mercury, we are forced to cast Teutatis as Mars, though the whole concept of war-god of the Celts as such may be an over-simplification. They never fought as a nation because they never were a nation. Usually they fought as tribes, sometimes in loose and unstable coalitions. One might, therefore, expect not one but many war-gods and there is evidence that this is the case. It accounts for the apparent confusion which seized the writers of the Gallo-Roman inscrip-tions, who in various places equate Mars not only with Teutatis, Esus, Cernunnos and Taranis, but also with such local deities as Cocidius, Rudiobus, Lenus, Corotiacus and Alator. But we know, in addition, that there were also powerful goddesses of war, like the Mórrígan. This apart, the most common translation of Teutatis is "God of the People" which would seem to make him something nearer to a giver of laws or a dispenser of justice.

Who then out of this list represents the "deified shaman" and hence the founder-god of the Celtic pantheon? In point of fact all have strong magical associations. Whether or not one is right in equating Esus with Mercury, we certainly know that the Roman god has a connexion with magic as the descendant of the Greek Hermes, who as Hermes Trimegistus, Hermes the Thrice-Great (a curiously Druidic-sounding epithet), supposedly provided the inspiration behind the "Hermetic system" used in alchemy, which later, taken over by orthodox science, was still being taken seriously as late as the time of Isaac Newton.

But Jupiter, equated wtih Taranis, is also a magician and sounds very much like a primal deity since his Latin name actually derives from "Father of the Gods".

But according to Dumezil, and the concept is elaborated by Eliade, the "magical king" is the "god who binds", that is to say who ties his worshippers to himself. In fact, one possible etymology of the word "religion" is through the verb 'religare', to tie together. The Hindu Varuna is associated with bonds in several of the Vedic hymns; so is the Norse Odinn, who on account of his ritual hanging of himself is sometimes called "God of the Rope" or "the Hanged". This would seem to give him a kinship with Esus in whose honour sacrificial victims were hanged and, in addition, there is equation often made between Odinn and Mercury.

Gods bear the marks of their creators and as Taranis, Esus and even Belenos are all super-magicians we can suppose their creators to have been magicians themselves, that is to say, the shamans or their successors the Druids.

But there is an even more convincing candidate for the role of "shaman-become-god" yet to be considered. This is Caesar's "Dispater", generally and most plausibly identified as Cernunnos. Strangely, he occurs less frequently than the other gods and is actually named only once, on an altar-stone found at Notre Dame de Paris. He has been tentatively identified, however, with a rock-carving in Val Camonica, Northern Italy and with representations found in Denmark, Rumania, Germany and Spain. At least one Celtic tribe appears to have derived its name from him and he may well be perpetuated in Cornwall, the Celtic name for which is Kernyw, as well as in such festivals as the Abbots Bromley stag-dance and the Breton *Pardon* of St. Cornely.

May he not also be the "Green Man" who in one form or other turns up with such regularity particularly in local legend?[1] One example may

---

[1]In this connexion there is a fascinating study to be made of British pub names. No far from Lewes in Sussex is a "Green Man" whose sign shows a head complete with horns. And how about some of

be Robin Hood, who traditionally wore green; there is a green giant in the Welsh *Dream of Rhonabwy*; while the festival of "The Lord of the Green Leaves" is kept by a community in Northumberland, described by Professor Ross, which still venerates the Celtic gods side by side with its Christian practices.

As Caesar tells us, it is he from whom the Gauls claim common descent, doing so by a "tradition preserved by the Druids". He is, on this evidence, a primary god.

He has been given the title of "Lord of the Animals" and the Gundestrup Cauldron shows him as squatting in the midst of various creatures. If one wished to represent the shaman surrounded by his animal-familiars, the Gundestrup picture is how one might well choose to do so. He even has his deer's antlers so that he may the better identify with them, as the shaman dresses himself in the likeness of that creature he seeks in spirit. Furthermore, he alone of the deities on the cauldron has eyes closed and wears the rapt expression of one entranced.

In his left hand he grasps his ram-headed serpent, but in his right he holds up what is indisputably an instrument of binding—a torc—while another encircles his own neck. The other gods on the cauldron's panels are similarly adorned, but it is Cernunnos alone who appears to be offering it. Thus, it may well be that the wearing of the torc, common to all classes of Celtic society may here have its origin. It was the symbol of their union with this all-important deity, who was father not only of mortals but also of the gods themselves. As a symbol of union, the wearing of a neck-ring is well-attested and is found, among other places, in the pre-Aryan cultures of India.

And if we pursue the Dumezilian vein further, there is another striking parallel. In terms of the space occupied on the cauldron, two gods predominate. The first is Cernunnos and his surrounding animals; the other, occupying the position facing him, is the one usually identified as Teutatis, the "God of the People" or "Ruler of the People", which seems to make him into Dumezil's "god of justice and the law". So once more we have the magical king opposed by the lawgiver as Varuna is opposed by Mitra or Odinn by Tyr.

But if he is so central to Druidism why are traces of Cernunnos less frequently found that those of other gods? Probably for this precise reason. To the Romans, out to expunge every vestige of Druidism, he would have seemed like its essence and, as they would no doubt have seen, since he was himself a kind of Other World Druid, none but the Druids could ever invoke or mediate with him. What the Romans began the early Christians would certainly have continued. It is usually

---

the others: The White Hart, to be found in almost every English town; The White Horse; or The Blue Boar?

accepted that he was the prototype of the Western image of Satan. There is no reason why Satan should have been given horns unless his likeness is based upon some model. This Cernunnos could certainly provide. He inhabited a subterranean Other World and he had strongly magical— that is to say, witchcraft—associations. Reasons enough to seek his total extirpation.

We can say with assurance that Cernunnos belongs to a group of deities which can be directly linked with Druidism, a group whose other members, on the intimations of Caesar, of the Gundestrup Cauldron, of the Berne *Scholia* and of their frequent recurrence over a wide area also included Belenos, Teutatis, Taranis and Esus, besides, no doubt, a powerful *Magna Mater*, probably in the form of a horse-goddess, Epona, with all the fertility cult practices normally associated with the worship of this type of deity. All six bear characteristics which indicate that they are primal gods whose origins reach down to the deepest levels of Celtic, or possibly of Indo-European pre-history. They were, therefore, a group of gods carried by the Celtic migrants to the lands in which they established themselves.

To their number were added the various tribal and territorial deities who form the greater proportion of that host we can ascribe to the Celts.

However, their establishment in their new territories along the Atlantic seaboard led the Celts to adopt a new strain of gods, so powerful and important that they were rapidly accorded parity with the original ones. These were the *Tuatha De Danann*, the people (or tribe) of the goddess Dana, that great family held to be the pre-Celtic deities of Ireland, but which were obviously taken over by Druidism and spread throughout the Celtic world. Indeed, the spread is such that one is forced to ask oneself whether there had not been some contact with the worshippers of the *Tuatha De Danann* long before their migrations to the British Isles. As we have seen, it was Celtic custom to associate powerful feminine deities with rivers; the more important the river, the more powerful the goddess linked with it. Among the two most important must have been the Danube, where the Celts first emerged, and the Marne, where the discoveries at La Tène indicate that there must have been a thriving society. The Marne derives from Matrona, The Mother; the Danube, mentioned by Herodotus about the middle of the 5th Century BC, has plain links with Danu (or Dana), *déesse-foundatrice* of the *Tuatha*, and mother-goddess par excellence, "the source," in the words of Markale, "of a race of gods and heroes". As the Welsh Don, she is, besides being mother of Math, the mother of Gilvaethy (Girflet in the Arthurian legends), of Arianrhod, mother of Lugh; of Amalthon the Labourer; of Hyveidd; and of the smith, Govannon, who is also the Irish Goibniu. So fertile is her womb that we can trace Cu Chulainn or even, with very little conjecture, Arthur back to it.

Admittedly controversy still surrounds the questions of whether Danu is one and the same as another goddess, Ana or Anu, but with the weight of opinion shifting forward the view that she was. A goddess called Anu is certainly to be found in Ireland where a hill in Kerry is called the "Paps of Anou" and she is especially associated with Munster. In Brittany, a mother-goddess called Ana survived as Saint Anne, its patron saint. It is generally asserted by Breton scholars that she was taken over from the pre-Celtic inhabitants of the peninsula. It accounts also for the wide distribution of St. Anne in place- and other names in Britain and elsewhere (the capital town of the Channel Island of Alderney, for example, is St. Anne's).

But we must not lose sight of another connexion: that between the two names Dana and Diana. In the latter, the first syllable may simply be an epithet meaning "god", in which case we would have something like "the goddess Ana". The cult of Diana, in origin a moon-deity, was extremely widespread in the ancient world and under the variants of her Greek name, Artemis, she goes back far into antiquity. She was to be found among the Etruscans who may themselves have borrowed her from Babylonic, certainly from Semitic, sources. Originally, she was associated with agriculture and hence with fertility, particularly that of women, though under the name Diana she was also the divine huntress, in which connexion a boar is one of her attributes (though, by name and in various other ways, Artemis is linked with the bear). The boar and huntresses are a recurrent motif of Celtic myth and iconography, occurring, among other places, on the partially defaced Ribchester stone dedicated to Maponos, "the Divine Son", and there are a number of Gallo-Roman inscriptions in which a local goddess is equated with Diana.

Her festival was on mid-summer's day June 24, and as we have seen, there are traces of customs practised on this day in both the Isle of Man and the Channel Islands. In the former, there is a direct, if tenuous link with Diana/Artemis in the wearing of mug-wort, *Artemisia vulgaris*, on St. John's Day, which is actually June 24. Throughout the Christian world, in the Middle Ages, St. John's Eve was an occasion for major festivity of a character singularly out of keeping with the somewhat austere nature of the Baptist himself, beheaded for refusing to moderate his condemnation of the incestuous King Herod. They included dancing in the streets, the lighting of public bonfires and, especially, uninhibited amatory displays by the young. It is hard to avoid the suspicion that the day corresponded with the festival of some important pagan deity, and this would help to explain why the church appointed it as the holy-day of one of its most august saints.

But who were the original invokers of the *Tuatha De Danann*? The generally accepted belief is that the pre-Celtic inhabitants of the British Isles were a people who had migrated from North Africa by way of the Atlantic seaboard of Europe, marking their progress by the building of the megaliths. For this, the myths themselves offer two interesting pieces of supportive evidence.

The first is the name of one of the central *Tuatha* deities, Lugh the Many Skilled. The Welsh form of his name, Lleu, means "lion" and that it was understood to mean this elsewhere is indicated by the name of the large French city Lyon, which derives from Lugdunum, "the fortress of Lugh". The use of "Y" to stand for the vowel-sound we today represent by "I" was no less common in Old French than in Old English, so that Lyon actually does mean "Lion". Lions are hardly creatures that the Indo-Europeans would have come into contact with and they would not, therefore, have taken one as a totem. On the other hand, they would certainly have been familiar enough to a people from North Africa.

The second piece of evidence is Diana/Artemis herself who, as we have already observed, undoubtedly had connexions with that general area. The Temple of Diana (actually, Artemis) at Ephesus was one of the Seven Wonders of the Ancient World and was still very much in use at the time of St. Paul.

But whether or not Dana/Ana is actually Diana, the fact remains that it is her offspring which figure most frequently and prominently in the myths. There are, to be sure, references in both those of Ireland and those of Wales which could be interpreted as hinting at the gods of the earlier phylum. In two of the Welsh stories, *Branwen Daughter of Llyr* and *How Culhwch Won Olwen* we have a Glinyeu ap Taran mentioned. There is also Beli the Great, son of Mynogan and Beli Adver, names certainly cognate with Belenos. Ross discusses a giant in the story of *The Lady of the Fountain* who, because of the power over animals he possesses, may be Cernunnos. Among the Irish stories, she suggests that he may lie concealed under the name of Conall Cernach in *The Driving-Off of Fraich's Cattle*. Here he displays power over serpents. This is congruous with the representation of Cernunnos on the Gundestrup Cauldron where he grasps a ram-headed serpent by the neck, but it also leads one to wonder whether St. Patrick's proverbial power over snakes may not, in fact, have had a pagan origin.

All these identifications have to be tentative, however, and the roles played in the stories are very subsidiary; sometimes they feature only as names in long lists. This is in contrast with the *Tuatha* deities: usually clearly labelled and playing key-roles. One must, naturally, take into account the confused state in which we have received the myths, though it would be very strange if the relegation of a group of important deities had been brought about by such inadvertence alone.

But we have, in addition, the evidence of the Christian festivals which were intended to supplant the earlier, pagan ones. Of these, two—the Feasts of Brigid and Lugh—both commemorate gods of the *Tuatha*, while almost all the myths surrounding Samain are associated with the same phylum of deities. The only exceptions are Beltain, the festival of Belenos, and the various, now purely local festivals traceable back to Cernunnos or, say, Epona, with the Padstow "Hobby-Horse" providing a good example. No surviving occasion can be traced to Esus, Teutatis or Taranis.

What was it about the life-style of the existing populations that so impressed the newly arrived Celts that they felt compelled to take over their gods? Undoubtedly it was the megaliths of which these aboriginals had been the builders, though even for them this had taken place in a past so remote that their constructors had ceased to be regarded as humans and had become gods.

Stories of the supernatural origins of the standing-stone are to be found wherever they occur. In the Channel Islands, particularly rich in them, the patois word, *"pouquelayé"*, means "puck or fairy" and not only does island folklore ascribe their building to these supernatural creatures (who are by no means to be conceived of as the tiny beings of later tradition), it also regards the stones as their dwelling-place which mortals disturb at their peril. In Brittany, down to late times, the stones were the centres of cults, probably pre-Celtic in origin.

We know, too, that the Celts were fascinated by them, burying their dead in megalithic tombs, absorbing them into their mythology as the *sidhs* and depositing round them what, in Piggott's words "looks like more than picnic debris". (There are also, incidentally, indications that some of the shafts and enclosures associated wih Druidism in Britain pre-date those of the Continent, offering support for Caesar's statement that Britain was the birthplace of the order.)

Among the megaliths were to be found, of course, the great stone circles, including the most astonishing of all—Stonehenge. From the work of Professor Gerald Hawkins and others it is now recognized that this is an astronomical computer, using a base of nineteen years (actually, $19+19+18=56$) to bring solar and lunar years into syncronization. From the Coligny calendar we also know this to have been the system employed by the Druids. It is, therefore, likely that they used Stonehenge (which would be consistent, anyway, with archaeological data from other henges where signs of Celtic use have been found) and they could only have learnt its complex operation under the tutelage of the existing priesthood.

We can now assert confidently that these Stone-Age people were themselves sophisticated astronomers which, as already pointed out, means they must also have possessed a quite high degree of mathematical skill.

In my view it was through their contacts with this priesthood, which may itself have had links with the same shaman-magicians who so greatly influenced the Persian Magi, Brahmins and Babylonic priesthood, that the Druids acquired the knowledge which led writers like Diogenes to equate them with these other three bodies.

In any event, discovering a system of religious belief so much more highly developed than their own, the Druids could scarcely ignore its deities. They had to be absorbed into their own pantheon. This must have posed a problem, for gods are notoriously jealous and do not take kindly to supersession or demotion. The solution the Druids adopted was that employed by others, notably the Greeks with their large and complex Olympus of interrelated deities: all the gods, new as well as old, became the members of one vast family or clan whose stories were encapsulated in a cycle of myths.

One finds oneself asking, in fact, whether anything recognizable as Druidism, at least as it impressed Aristotle and, through him, Diogenes can actually have existed before this time.

Nonetheless, whatever the original personalities of the gods of this influx may have been, they would quickly have acquired the likeness of the people who were worshipping them.

The life of the gods differed little from that of men. They tilled the land like Amathaon or they wrought metal into weapons like Govannon. They feasted and they fornicated. They knew the pangs of desire and did not scruple to use any subterfuge to satisfy it.

Yet these activities merely filled the intervals of peace between the great battles in which they participated with the same rumbustious joy in violence as men. For them, it was no more than a game, played according to its own strict code of rules and none the worse because the stakes were the highest of all. And the gods, too, could suffer in the fray. Nuada lost his hand, and even death was no stranger. Carman died as a prisoner in the hands of the *Tuatha De Danann*. Brân survived decapitation as a disembodied head. He and his seven companions lived a life of joyous feasting which lasted eighty years, before the head was finally laid to rest at White Hill in London.

What distinguished the divine from the human, then? The power of magic, naturally, and Ross has drawn attention to the expression of "withdrawn, inscrutable intensity" which characterizes almost all depictions of deities, even those which, artistically, are the most rudimentary. Nowhere is this more marked than on the faces which decorate the

Gundestrup Cauldron. Yet they were capable of compassion, as well. When Cu Chulainn is wounded, Lugh, visible only to his favourite, comes to his side and not only comforts him and dresses his wounds, he even undertakes to replace him on the battlefield so that his forces' strength will not be depleted by his absence.

The gods were marked off from mere humans, all the same.

One of the archaeological mysteries surrounding the Celts is the frequent occurrence of "Janus" heads, that is to say heads made up of two or more, often three, faces. There are a number of possible explanations for this. One is that three was the sacred number of the Druids. Much of their learning is expressed in "triads". It is also possible that the three faces represent three aspects of the god. Thus, the triple representations of Macha, the Irish horse-goddess, is explained as being due to the fact that woman has three aspects: the mother, the virgin and "the devourer of men".

Powell suggests that this tricephalism expressed the idea that the gods were conceived as "to the power of three". That is to say they had in all things thrice the power of men.

This undoubtedly applied to their stature. Hence we find the hillside figures as giants. Interestingly enough, the Cornish giant Gogmagog is described as being twelve cubits tall. This is equivalent to eighteen feet or three times the height of a tall man. And the Celts were themselves tall. Other nations saw them as a race of giants so that Diodorus ascribes the foundation of the Celtic nation to Hercules. They could hardly have seen themselves other than as large and, indeed, they attributed their military invincibility to this physical advantage.

Esteeming large stature, one would expect their gods to be giants. And this is how we find them. On the Gundestrup Cauldron they dwarf both mortals and animals. In the Welsh stories we constantly come across supernatural giants, Ysbaddaden in *How Culhwch Won Olwen*; the green giant, Iddawg in *The Dream of Rhonabwy*; the black giant in *Owein*. Brân carried musicians on his back across the water separating Ireland and Wales. From Ireland we have the god Dagda copulating with the Mórrígan with one foot on either bank of a river, while rivers themselves result from the urination of goddesses. Scottish legend, too, is replete with its giant gods.

It may well be that it is in the light of this we should interpret the sacrificial colossi in the image of a man mentioned by Caesar and Strabo.

And who could have built the megaliths but giants? No wonder the gods of Druidism as we see them represented look out on puny mortals with their cool, dispassionate gaze. The wonder is that they can be coerced into interesting themselves in the affairs of these mannikins at all.

A tradition associating the megaliths with giants is particularly persistent. In Geoffrey of Monmouth's *History of the Kings of Britain*, the British king Aurelius decides to set up a monument to those fallen in battle against the Saxon marauders. Merlin prevails upon him to fetch a group of enormous, magical stones from Ireland. These form, so Merlin tells him, 'The Giants Ring', and they were erected by titans, who brought them from Africa, at the time they ruled Ireland.

CHAPTER NINE

Doctrine: the Myth of Rebirth

NOW that we have gone some way in forming an idea of the Druidic pantheon, can we hope to find a unitary system of belief, something which we can properly speak of as "Druidism", as we speak of Buddhism or Hinduism?

Caesar mentions the belief in transmigration of the soul and interprets it as a means of inculcating fearlessness in battle as, in Celtic society, it must have been. Kendrik refers to it as the sole Druidic doctrine to come down to us and this view is echoed, more or less, by most other writers. Even Markale, in his essay on the topic, confesses to the difficulty of reconstructing a "Druidic" philosophy and what he himself has been able to piece together is couched in negative rather than positive terms. They did not, for example, accept the duality of Good and Evil, but understood their own lives and the universe itself as being guided by a single internal movement. There was, in consequence, no concept of reward or punishment in an afterworld.

Piggott mentions a triad quoted by Diogenes Laertius as the summary of Druidic ethical teaching which bids believers to worship the gods, refrain from evil and maintain manly conduct. This is so all-embracing that there can hardly be a single creed to which it could not with slight modification, be applied. Much the same goes for the quotation from the Irish 12th Century *Colloquy of the Elders*. Here St. Patrick, in an imaginary dialogue with the pagan hero, Caelte, is told that he and his people were sustained in life by "the truth that was in our hearts, the strength in our arms and the fulfilment in our tongues". This might come marginally closer to the sort of view one might expect from a member of a vigorous, heroic society, but it helps not at all in distinguishing Druidic doctrine from others.

Strabo mentions the belief that the universe, like men's souls, was indestructible, "but that fire and water will sometime or other prevail over them".

The truth is surely that the quest for an underlying doctrinal base is a vain one. Not even the classical religions can yield anything remotely resembling it. The most they offer is that honouring the gods will bring its own reward, and in general attitudes towards them are those summed up in Shakespeare's epigram, "As flies to wanton boys are we to the gods ... " Even Tacitus can say only, "As to the acts of the gods, it seems holier and more reverent to believe than to know".

We must remind ourselves that the Druids are the direct descendants of shamans and that shamanism is not concerned with broad issues of causality, with rules of conduct applicable to all men. Certainly, there is no question of that subjection of human to divine will which to our eyes would be the hallmark of religion. They are concerned with the specific instance: the means whereby the hunter can secure his prey and protect himself from the malignity of its spirit; the banishing of whatever occult forces are causing the particular illness or, say, an epidemic among his cattle.

The "spirits" are, as I M Lewis says, "amoral". They visit with affliction or grant favour without consideration of the character or conduct of the recipient. The same must go for the gods of the Druids as for those of similar cultures. In the Norse legend of the king "magically" sacrificed when the calf's-gut round his neck becomes a rope, we are given no hint that such a fate was deserved. Odinn has simply demanded repayment for his gift to Starkad and this is how he takes it. There are several parallels in Celtic myth.

It is only by means of ritual that men have the slightest chance of safeguarding themselves from the caprices of spirits or gods. This explains why it is even more essential to magic than religion. For religion ritual is a pure symbol: the smoke of incense rising skywards symbolizes the petitions of the faithful rising to the throne of God; it is not, of itself, those petitions. Magic's rituals, when performed correctly in every minutest detail, are per se effective. Their sole aim is to compel the obedience of those forces towards which they are directed.

From the Isle of Man comes the story of the lazy wife, one of several such to be found all over the Celtic world. Too idle to spin the wool her husband brings her, she one days receives a surprise visit from a giant. He undertakes to help her if she can only guess his name which, after several attempts, she does. By his sudden appearance, so typical of Celtic Other World beings, her visitor had made his true nature clear. The woman calls him, nonetheless, "Mollyn droat"—"the servant of the Druid"—and in that attitude sums up an entire attitude to deities.

Thanks to the work of T C Lethbridge we can now be sure that the giant, chalk-cut figures adorning so many of our hillsides are not only far more numerous than was previously supposed, but also that they are connected with Druidism—strangely enough similar ones are also to be found in India. The male figure at Cerne Abbas in Dorset is probably the Celtic Hercules, Ogmios, for example. The female horse-rider un-covered by Lethbridge at Wandlebury in Cambridgeshire has been identified by Sir Cyril Fox as Epona and the Uffington White Horse may also be a representation of her. The purpose of such figures can only have been, surely, the ritual one of "fixing" something of the divine essence upon the locality in which they are portrayed, in the same man-ner as the cave-artists of Lascaux or Schmidt's pygmy-hunter tried to "fix" the spirits of their quarries by their creations. As Frazer and others have pointed out, any representation is thought of as containing some part of the vital force of the original. It is for this very reason that natives in some remote areas will go to such lengths to avoid being photo-graphed.

In much the same way the fertility of the land is ritually "guaranteed" when the territorial goddess is given her mortal mate, the new king.

Illness, too, is cured, not by any property inherent in the herb, but by the entire spell wrought over the "spirit" causing the illness, from the moment of gathering to its application to the patient. So Pliny tells us that in gathering *selago* (no translation has ever been agreed), it was necessary for the Druids involved to wear white robes and to stretch their right hands through the left sleeve "in the manner of a thief". Similar attitudes were held by the herb-doctors found until recently in the Channel Islands and still existing in the Isle of Man, where their treatments were so esteemed that the island legislature had to abandon a measure to control the practice of medicine because it would have abolished them. These practitioners, often spoken of as "the last of the Druids", insisted that one must never speak of picking, but always of "lifting" and that this must be done with a charm. The same lifting would not serve for more than one patient. For maximum therapeutic effect nine pieces of a herb were necessary, then seven, six might serve and in cases where the plant was rare one might even use three—all, of course, are magical numbers.

In Jersey, there were similarly detailed prescriptions for the use of herbs. Among those most highly prized were vervain; L'Amy speaks of it as the "holy herb of the Druids", which besides being a panacea for all maladies, can break the spells of sorcerers and reconcile enemies. In its lifting care had to be taken to see not a single fibre of the root remained in the soil. A piece of the root was then cut off and hung round the patient's neck with a ribbon, while the rest of it was burnt. The foliage was hung on a chimney and, as it dried, the illness would disappear.

But quite apart from the essentially magical character of Druidism, the abstraction of ethical principles from its only "statement"—the myths—would have the effect of making them something other than what, to the eyes of the Celts as to other similar societies, they were. They would then become religious allegory, and they were nothing of the kind. The myth exists autonomously. It is not the retelling of events; it is the programme of the events themselves.

To understand this we have to understand that the conception of time held by many cultures, of which the Celtic was certainly one, was quite different from our own. Some hint of this is given in the old opening formula of the fairy-story: "Once upon a time ... " The Breton story tellers, according to Markale, went still further, for they began: "Once upon a time, there was no time, and it was then that ... " Thus there are not one but many "times" of which the "progressive" one known to us, that of irreversible change, is only one version.

But in contrast with this one, with events passing in an unending cavalcade, there was that one in which it was the observer himself who passed events, cyclically, in the same way that, for example, while sitting on a roundabout one might see a couple embracing and catch them repeatedly, frozen in their attitudes, with each revolution of the machine. Here events were recoverable or could be "revisited" and this was the time inhabited by the gods. It could be partly shared by their human intermediaries in trance—a sense of being "outside time" is a characteristic of this state. The rest of the human race came nearest to it only during the rituals of the high festivals.

Since myth is the event itself there can be no place for the kind of extrapolation which doctrine represents. The frequent visits of mythical heroes to the Other World, so constant a motif of, for example, the Welsh stories, are indicative only of the close intermeshing of mortal and immortal existences. Notwithstanding the evidence that the advance on Delphi partook in some degree of the character of just such an expedition to the Other World, it should not be supposed that these ventures were enjoined upon the faithful in the way that Muslims are enjoined to visit Mecca.

And so we are left with transmigration as the central and one persisting tenet of doctrine. In fact, as Max Weber makes clear, it is also the only discernible one in Brahminism, and in both cases it is obviously little more than a development of the shaman's image of a world haunted by the souls of the envious dead liable to take up their abode in the bodies of the living.

The difficulty lies in discovering the exact scope and form of a belief which, after all, is common to many religions (though usually traceable back to shamanistic sources). Its variations are as wide as those of the religions themselves. In some, the soul is said to move freely from human to animal habitation; in others, it always occupies a human body; in others, the cycle of birth-death-rebirth continues until redemption and Nirvana have been achieved; in still others, it lasts perpetually.

If we can trust Lucan, who speaks of the Druids as viewing death as "but the mid-point in a long-life", there seems to be the implication that men live, as it were, a double life. But there is no other reliable sanction for this.

Did it apply to all? Kendrick believed that survival was enjoyed only by the warrior-aristocracy and this seems to be the view taken by Markale. "It is only possible to declare." he says, "that there are certain examples of reincarnation in the Celtic myths, but always limited to certain persons. " If, however, it was, as Caesar says, intended to overcome fear of death among warriors, then it must have been extended further, though we have no warrant for suggesting it was conditional, say, on death in battle.

Perhaps a clue to the nature of the belief lies at the other terminal of existence, birth, no less mysterious than death itself. We have already seen that the Celts, at least in the earliest times, had no concept of the male role in conception. In these circumstances, one explanation of pregnancy and birth would be that it came about through spirits taking up habitation in the uterus, a belief still held among some Pacific islanders.

But we have, as a matter of fact, fairly plain hints about the means by which, in Druidic belief, the spirit was thought to enter the womb: in *The Wooing of Etain*, Etain Echraide is abducted by the *sidh*-god Midir. Unfortunately there is already a woman installed in Midir's palace, the sorceress, Fuamnach, who takes Etain's arrival very much amiss and in a fit of jealousy changes her into a blue-bottle. First chased out to sea, she manages to fly back to land, where exhausted and battered by the winds, she finally lands on the roof of a house and falls through the smoke-hole into a cup. The house is, by chance, that of the king of Ulster whose wife, taking a drink from the cup, swallows the fly. In due course, she becomes pregnant and bears a daughter who is Etain regenerate.

Nessa, mother of King Conchobḥar, becomes pregnant after drinking water given to her by her husband, the Druid, Cathbadh. In the story of the begetting of the magic bulls of Cooley, who later became the object of the raid, we first encounter them as the two swineherds of rival *sidh*-kings, Ochall Ochne and Bodb. Dismissed when their pigs fail to fatten, the swineherds spend two years as birds of prey, then return to their original shapes; next they spend two years as water-creatures, living under the sea, then they become two stags, then warriors, then phantoms, then dragons and finally maggots which drop into a stream to be drunk by two cows, to whom they are reborn as the two bulls, Finntbennach Ai, the white and Donn Cuailnge, the brown.

The Irish bard, Tuan mac Cairll, like his Welsh counterpart, Taliesin, undergoes many metamorphoses in which he becomes, inter alia, a stag, a boar, a hawk and a salmon, and in this form is eaten by the wife of Cairill to be reborn in his ultimate shape.

In the case of Taliesin, the transformations are even more elaborate, as is told in a comic story. Kerridwen, wife of Tegi Voel of Penllyn, gives birth to a boy of such ugliness she decides, in compensation, to equip him with knowledge such as cannot fail to impress all who meet him. From the *Books of Fferyllt*, she discovers the recipe for a magical liquid which will impart inspiration and knowledge. The reference to the *Books of Fferyllt*, which means "a worker in metal", introduces a touch of alchemy, a theme pursued in the story. The liquid must distill for a year and a day until only three potent drops remain. This long process is tended by Gwyon Bach and the blind Morda. All goes well until almost the end and, when Gwyon spills a little of the hot liquid on his finger and, because of the pain, puts it to his mouth. He at once receives the enlightenment intended for Kerridwen's son, and realizing what he has done, flees. Now guarded only by Morda, the cauldron in which the magic liquid has been brewing bursts and the last of the precious subtance is lost.

An irate Kerridwen sets out to find Gwyon, who thanks to the ingestion of the liquid is able to change himself at will. He therefore becomes a hare the more easily to escape, but Kerridwen outwits him by becoming a greyhound. Gwyon then throws himself into a river and becomes a fish; again, Kerridwen trumps him: she becomes an otter. Gwyon responds by becoming a bird; Kerridwen, a falcon. At last, Gwyon turns himself into a grain of corn. In vain, for Kerridwen becomes a black hen and devours it. She duly becomes pregnant, but when the infant is born, she cannot bring herself to kill it, as she intended. Instead, she puts it into a bag of skin which she consigns to the waters. In due course, the bag is found by Elffin, son of Gwyddno, who saves the child and brings him up under the name of Taliesin.

In other words, as is plain from all these stories, regeneration occurs when a woman consumes the "spirit" which has been transformed into some suitable form.

The cauldron which here serves Kerridwen for alembic no doubt comes into the story more or less by chance. The cauldron was after all the principal cooking pot of the times. That it also served ritual functions is clear not only from the Gundestrup Cauldron, but from the numerous references in myth. In the *mabinogi* of *Manawydan Son of Llyr*, Pryderi, while hunting a magic white boar, comes upon a mysterious castle which his dogs, following the scent, enter. Pryderi, against Manawydan's advice, follows. In a magnificent interior court, he sees a golden bowl hanging by chains over a marble slab. He attempts to take it, but when he grasps it his hands stick to it and his feet to the marble slab, while he also loses the power of speech. The queen, Rhiannon, who goes in search of him, is similarly afflicted when she tries to grasp the bowl.

The storyteller goes on: "When the night came thunder rolled and a mist fell; the fortress vanished it, and they with it".

The castle is obviously a *sidh* and the incident represents yet another visit to the Other World. The story has undergone considerable redaction by scribes who had no idea of its deeper meaning. One likely change made by them was in the story's ending, since the present one introduces a bishop. A little light is cast when one recalls that Rhiannon is the Welsh equivalent of Epona/Macha, the horse-goddess, who is also a Great Mother, and that Pryderi may be Maponos who, of course, also appears in a boar-hunt in the story of Culhwch and is connected with hunting in the Ribchester altar-stone mentioned earlier. Maponos is often equated with Appolo, the sun-god, and this would certainly make sense of the golden bowl which the god and his mother try to repossess. Furthermore, the owner of the castle is Llwyd, which means gray, and the basic problem of the story is to discover the cause of a mysterious desolation which has fallen upon the land. The myth then is about the theft of the golden-bowl of the sun by the gray *sidh*-god of winter.

One important element is the fact that both Pryderi and Rhiannon are struck dumb by contact with the bowl. There are similarities in two other cauldron-myths. The cauldron which Brân attempts to steal from the Irish has the property that if one took "a man who has been slain today and throw him into it . . . . tomorrow he will fight as well as ever, only he will not be able to speak". The cauldron which Peredur is shown in the court of the King of Suffering is also used to restore the dead to life.

The cauldron's life-giving properties are, of course, shared by the sun, which after the gray desolation of winter quickens the dead seed.

It is this which connects it with transmigration, for Diodorus, drawing on Posidonius, tells that the Celts believe that when they died "after a definite number of years they live a second life when the soul passes to another body". In other words, there is between one life and another a period of fallowness, analogous to winter.

The similarity of the uterus to a cauldron is hardly one which could have escaped Celtic notice, if only because a woman in the final stages of pregnancy looks very much as if she had a bowl inside her. There are, to be sure, the numerous rustic jokes on the subject to be found almost everywhere in which an expectant woman is described as carrying a cooking pot, pitcher or something similar under her skirts.

One might hazard, therefore, that the Druidic doctrine of transmigration could be restated somewhat along these lines:

> Plants grow, flower and fruit through the summer. But *sidh*-god of winter seizes the magic bowl of the sun which gives them life and takes it to his castle, whereupon everything withers and dies. However, in death the plant drops its seeds upon the earth. Here it would remain, a dead thing were it not for the sun-god's courage. While hunting he is led by the magic boar (note the beneficent, totemic animal) to the winter-god's castle, which he bravely enters and where aided by his great mother, he repossesses the golden bowl, though not without many perilous adventures. When it returns to its proper place in the sky, the seed is quickened into life and the plant lives again.
>
> It is the same with men. As their winter comes and with it, death, their seed also falls, to remain in the Underworld until it is, under some guise, devoured by a woman to enter the cauldron of resurrection in her belly.

As the explanation of birth, these ideas would obviously have been modified as the male role came to be understood. (As we know, at this stage the man sees his own and not the woman's, function as the all-important one. His is the seed; she the mere soil into which it is implanted. From this stems patrilinear descent and with it the dominance of the male.) However, the idea would no doubt have persisted in myth where it would be seen as an example of "miraculous-birth" imbuing the child involved with supernatural qualities.

But could we, perhaps, have here the rudiments of an answer to another problem; the reason for the Celtic practice of severing heads? The custom is well-attested not only in the classical descriptions of the Celts, but also archaeologically and in myth down to late times. Herodotus describes their being set up on high staves, "so that the head sticks up far above the house, often above the chimney". He was told that it served thereby as "guardian of the whole house".

Archaeology has unearthed skulls in votive deposits, niches for them in buildings, stone and wooden representations of heads (all with a most uncanny look of death about them), as well as sculptured masonry, like the pillar at Entremont, Bouches du Rhône, whose principal sculpture was disembodied heads. Professor Ross has gone so far as to suggest that the adornment of houses and other buildings with representations of the human head, as for example in gargoyles or overarches, is a survival of the practice.

It occurs in Scottish, Irish and Welsh myth—in the story of *Gereint and Enid*, for example, Gereint is about to behead an enemy but has his handed stayed. Among the numerous references in the Arthurian legend is that in Chrêtien de Troyes's version to *The Maiden of the Mule*, who demands from Lancelot the head of a recently slain enemy. When he gives it to her she evinces the greatest gratitude, promising to aid him whenever he is in need.

In folk custom there are the numerous curative wells, some of which, like *Tobar na Ceann* in the Outer Hebrides, actually have the word "head" in their names, while others have saints' names.

In former days many of these had a skull, said to be that of the saint, standing by them for use as a drinking vessel. This connects with references in both Herodotus and Livy to skulls used as goblets.

Herodotus tells us that the cranium was sawn off above the eyebrows, the interior cleaned and the exterior covered in calf-leather, if the owner were poor, or lined in gold if he were rich. Livy cites the example of the chief of the Boii, who, after capturing the Roman consul Postumius, had his skull gold-mounted and used it as a cup.

The examples of skulls dropped into wells and particularly their use for drinking water from curative wells, by associating them, in one way or another, with health or its restoration, also, of course, link them with the maintenance of life itself. But, like the seed head of a plant, standing at the plant's top, so the head and the skull tops the man. It is his "seed-head", the place where the potential for life resides. In the shamanic spirit flights, in the legends surrounding such ecstasy-cults as that of the Pythian Apollo, as well as in some found in Tibet and China, even in contemporary reports of so-called "out-of-the-body" experiences the spirit is said to leave and enter the body via the head.

By taking possession of an enemy's head, therefore, one can ensure that he is not reborn to seek revenge, but at the same time, because of its potential for life, it also has health-giving properties of its own.

There is still, however, one aspect of the teaching of transmigration which requires examination. This is the all important Druidic notion of equilibrium, another idea found in early Brahminism and even in ancient Chinese systems, which it seems to have entered by way of Taoism, itself strongly influenced by shamanism. In Celtic terms the notion is well illustrated in one of the Welsh stories, that of Peredur, who is the most likely prototype for Sir Percival or Parsifal in the later versions of the Arthurian legends.

While out adventuring, the young knight comes upon a very strange sight. He passes through a wooded valley, bisected by a river. On either bank, sheep graze, but those on the one bank are white, while those on the other are black. Whenever one of the white sheep bleats, one of the black wades through the river to emerge on the other side, white: whenever one of the black sheep bleats, a white sheep goes through the same process to arrive, black, on the far bank. That the river represents the divide between the world of living and dead is plain enough. It is a symbol to be found in many rivers from the Greek Styx to the Christian Jordan. The story makes it quite explicit, however, for on the river's bank there also stands a tree, one half of which is green with leaves, while the other half is aflame "from roots to crown".

The black and white sheep, then, represent the dead and the living respectively. One may hazard that the two remain roughly in balance, for, since they could summon one another, each could ensure that his numbers did not diminish. The world of living and dead are, therefore, inextricably bound one with another. When the transmigrating soul is summoned from the world of death to take up abode among the living once more, the world of the dead will, sooner or later, make its summons, too.

One would, of course, expect this concept to have some bearing on the practice of human sacrifice, indeed to provide a rationale for it. And, turning to Caesar, one finds this is the case. As an illustration of the extreme superstition of the Gauls, he tells us that those "suffering from serious disease, as well as those who are exposed to perils of battle, offer or vow to offer, human sacrifices, for the performance of which they employ the Druids". Thus, when the black sheep bleat, those of the white sheep who have reason to feel the call most likely to apply to them, try to find a substitute.

Conversely, birth itself is also a matter for awe, as this summoning of the black sheep to join the white will demand its requital.

CHAPTER TEN

The Blood Soaked Altars

THE notion of consigning a living human to a cruel and bloody death amid the trappings of religious observance is, of course, one to which a whole gamut of conflicting emotions attach themselves, including a kind of macabre, almost shameful fascination, which in those cases where we learn that the victims were young girls is not unmixed with sexual overtones. Eros and Thanatos often walk hand in hand, and one thinks of the young bloods of revolutionary France, bribing prison warders to allow them to sleep with condemned aristocratic beauties on the night before they went to the guillotine.

The practice comes into the category of things only half credible. "Could people really have carried out such acts upon one another?", we find ourselves asking; and, having convinced ourselves, find its grotesqueness such that we feel it must have had its reflection in the temperament and attitudes of the people practising it. It must, somehow, have influenced their relations with one another. Would they not have eyed strangers in a special, terrifying way, considering their acceptability as offerings to the gods, as we might expect cannibals to weigh them up with a view to the choicer cuts?

Considerations of this kind certainly entered the minds of the Spaniards on their way to the newly conquered South and Central Americas. It is plain that it gave a little frisson to the Romans, as they read the various accounts of Celtic activities in this sphere.

Yet in their expression of disapproval both Spaniards and Romans were guilty of applying a double standard.

The Spanish travellers came from a society where the torture chamber (unknown to the Aztecs and Incas) and the *autos da fe* operated under Papal blessing. Tacitus, throwing up hands of horror at the Druids' human sacrifices, conveniently overlooked the fact that his own countrymen wantonly massacred infinitely greater numbers with the purely frivolous objective of titillating the mob at the circus than ever the Druids sacrificed. Caesar, in his efforts to curry popularity, was himself responsible for having the Circus Maximus expensively rebuilt and there inaugurating an era of hideously blood-thirsty spectacles. By contrast, the Celts could claim for their activities the serious purpose of sustaining the cycle of existence.

And, come to that, human sacrifice had been practised by both Rome and Greece. Euripides' play *Iphigenia in Aulis* treats the subject, here with Agamemnon's daughter as victim and father as sacrificer, as high tragedy. There is every indication that the play was well received; no one seemed to question its basic premise. In Rome, the practice of human sacrifice had been ended officially only in the early years of the 1st Century BC. It follows that in Caesar's lifetime there must have been at least some who remembered it. Even by Tacitus's day it had been abolished barely 150 years. Roman abhorrence can only have been the holier-than-thou attitude of the recently converted.

And if we ourselves feel able to indulge in self-congratulation, we ought to remember how short a time it is since we took human life in conditions whose ritualistic overtones included the presence of a priest. The more one contemplates judicial execution, the more like a relic of human sacrifice does it become.

In the case of the Druids, nonetheless, it arouses in many people not only revulsion, but also incomprehension. If one can justly ascribe to them a fairly sophisticated practical knowledge and an involvement in a creative life which, at least in the cases of their art and literature, which we know of, were of surpassing brilliance and sensitivity, how could they have given themselves to such practices? It is understandable, therefore, that some of the more idealizing writers have sought to exculpate the Druids from participation, suggesting that in so far as they were present it was only as reluctant bystanders.

This is as frankly implausible as those theories which try to justify human sacrifice in terms of concepts like "rebirth", as per Eliade, or those which see the victim as a kind of messenger, a mediator, dispatched to the realm of the gods on behalf of his people.

The first draws its justification from such concepts as the symbolical death and rebirth in Christian baptism or that undergone by the novice-shaman in his search for enlightenment. The fact is that symbolical death is one thing, the actual annihilation of the physical person whereby he becomes, observably, changed into a motionless carcase, quite another.

And as to the second, one wonders what kind of mediation on behalf of those responsible for his slaughter could have been expected from the wretches stuffed into their wicker cages to be incinerated or from the prisoners-of-war whose heads were held down in a basin of water until they suffocated—both methods we know to have been practised.

Anyway, the Druids, as successors of the shamans probably had no need of mediators: they were perfectly able to visit the divine realms themselves.

And the truth is that there is absolutely nothing in Druidism to give sanction to the supposition that they carried out sacrifice for such reasons. The victims of the wicker colossi were, of course, condemned criminals and examples of sacrifice as capital punishment are not lacking. In Scandinavia, in the period in which Christianity and paganism co-existed in different areas, observers of heathen customs record that criminals were frequently "condemned to be sacrificed".

It is, however, invariably a symptom of human sacrifice in decline and this may well have been the case with Druidism in the years up to the Roman conquest of Gaul and Britain.

By the time of Pomponius Mela (circa AD 40) it had become vestigial, at least in Gaul, with a kind of symbolical nicking of the victim standing for his slaughter. We cannot, of course, be sure how matters stood elsewhere, but one Irish story records that through divine intervention, a cow was substituted for a human victim, as the ram was substituted for Isaac in the Biblical story of Abraham, which is itself usually taken to be a mythical representation of the abandonment of human sacrifice by the Hebrews. Furthermore, while the early Christian missionaries disapproved of such superstitious practices of Druidism as divination, there is nothing about human sacrifice, a practice they could hardly have condoned had they found it.

Admittedly, it is likely that some forms persisted down to late times and we have a legend in which St. Columba himself supposedly employed something akin to it! Nevertheless, in general, any discussion of it must hark back to a time when the Druids were at the height of their powers, a time of which because of its remoteness we know least, so that much remains conjectural.

This applies, for example, to the actual modes of dispatch of which we have only the sketchiest details. It is the Berne *Scholiasts*, in their commentary on the *Pharsalia*, who tell us that those offered up to Teutatis had their heads held down in a pot of water, while those offered to Esus were suspended head down from the limbs of trees, then stabbed. Some authorities believe that they were actually beheaded, but the whole practice may, in fact, be one of those occasions in which the so-called "triple death" was applied. In its best known form the victim was put in a building which was then set on fire. As he tried to escape he was recaptured, had his head held under water and was finally stabbed.

It has been pointed out by several scholars that the principal methods of sacrifice—those of burning, drowning and hanging—correspond with the three elements of the ancient world, fire, water and earth which also associates it with alchemy. The references to stabbing may possibly connect with the methods used in taking auspices, since, according to the *Scholia*, in the case of the sacrifices to Esus omens were drawn from the flow of blood. It is more likely, however, that it was simply conceived of as nourishment for the ground.

In other descriptions, we are told that methods of sacrifice included impalement in a temple (or, presumably, in a sacred grove) as well as shooting with arrows.

Little more than oblique hints of sacrifice are given in the Irish and Welsh texts. There is mention, for instance, of the *bruidne*, burning buildings in which people are destroyed. These occur in the Irish *Intoxication of the Ulstermen* and *The Destruction of Ding Rig* as well as in the Welsh *Branwen Daughter of Llyr*, though here the relevant part of the story actually takes place in Ireland.

Another form of sacrifice is encountered in a Connaught story. This tells how a maiden had many wooers and how for each suitor a person was chosen from among his community and, at Samain, secretly killed. Not much interpretative skill is required to understand that the "maiden" is a goddess and that each community of her worshippers provided one sacrificial victim. Clandestine killing is a theme repeatedly found in Druidic practice, where kings, for example, were often disposed of in this way.

In other, admittedly less reliable contexts, children and cattle are described as being offered at Samain, though Pliny confirms that animal sacrifices were carried out.

One of the first things to emerge in any study of sacrifice, whether the victims are human or animal, is that it is by no means the product of primitive reasoning processes making crude links between cause and effect and, as a result, seeking to placate divine anger or secure its favour much as one would with a powerful human—with offering of what one most valued. It is an act carried out from such a variety of motives that the all-embracing term "sacrifice" with its special connotations for us, is quite inadequate to comprehend them.

Nor should we suppose that in all cases where a human being dies in a ritual context we are entitled to speak of sacrifice. In some instances, the slaying of the king looks very much more like a means of ridding his community of a liability than an offering intended to please. From Strabo and Diodorus we know, of course, of the Druidic technique of divination involving the stabbing of a man in the midriff and the taking of auspices from the flowing of blood and his death throes. Among the later alchemists human blood was often prescribed for transmutations. The Medieval infanticide, Gilles de Rais, condemned to death in 1440, gave details of such practices in a voluntary confession. One can reasonably suppose that the Druids, themselves magicians who may well have practised something like alchemy, also had formulae calling for human blood.

That placation and tribute were among the reasons for sacrifice, there can be no argument. The offering of kings might be an example of one; that of prisoners taken in war, of the other, for Caesar tells us that it was Celtic custom to devote the spoils of the battlefield to their gods. Even in the case of the punishment of criminals by burning it is also part of justification: Strabo says that when there was "a big yield" (of criminals) it was believed that there would also be "a big yield from the land". The gift, in other words, looked for its return.

But there was, besides, the principle of equilibrium already examined and this, too, seems to have been present in the last example, since Caesar declares that if insufficient convicts were available, the Druids did "not hesitate to make up with innocent men". But again, we must remember that this was probably a time when the practice was degenerating.

At the peak of Druidic power and influence, however, there was one form of sacrifice which was unarguably central: that in which the victim was conceived as becoming the divinity invoked. It was by no means an exclusively Celtic concept, for it is to be found as the rason d'être behind the practice almost wherever it occurs; certainly among those about whose human sacrificial practices we know most – the Aztecs and Incas. One can go so far as to declare that without it human sacrifice is indeed what it is commonly conceived to be – a cruel, barbaric formality.

Properly to fulfil its ritual function, sacrifice requires a compliant victim. In the case of Caesar's description this appears to be absent, even if we accept that his information was up-to-date, and it may well not have been.

The various references to secret stabbings would indicate that here, too, complicity was not anticipated, and there are signs that the choice of victim or his avoidance of his fate had become the subject of something like a lottery. In some part of Ireland there is a surviving custom in which participants dance in a circle round an oatcake which stands on a stump of wood. At the climax of the dance the cake is broken up and shared. In pagan times, however, one corner of it was burnt and whoever received it was settled upon as the victim. By contrast, a Beltain custom in the Orkney and Shetland isles, also found in the Scottish Highlands, was for young men to leap through the flames of the fires. This apparent act of bravado derives from a method by which the victim could save himself. If he jumped six times through the blaze he was reprieved.

Both practices indicate reluctance on the part of the victims and are at odds with what we know of earlier times among the Celts, as well as what we find in other cultures.

Just outside the city of Chichen Itza in what is now Yucatan, is a small lake. From the mud of its bed some thousands of small skulls have been dredged by archaeologists, those of young children, offered to the god of the waters. One could expect the scene of slaughter to have been made hideous by screams, terror and pitiable struggles of the little victims. It was nothing of the kind, as we know from contemporary evidence. Fully aware of their fate, they led the procession from the city to the rampart overhanging the waters, proud and erect, singing the hymns in praise of the god to whom they were to be immolated. Once there, they stretched out their bodies on the altar-stone to receive the knife's thrust.

Almost every account of Aztec sacrifice demonstrates not merely acquiescence on the part of victims, but full and free cooperation. Offered the chance of avoiding their fate, most, far from embracing it, declined. The woman chosen as offering to the maize-god put on her elaborate sacrificial robes and jewellery, made up her face with ochre and carmine in imitation of the growing corn, while friends fluttered about her, helping her as they would help a bride dressing for her wedding. When all was ready she led the public celebration, the singing and the dancing which for her ended as she entered the temple and her head was struck from her body.

We have not the slightest reason to suppose it was any different with the Celts in fully pagan times. As Powell comments, there is little doubt that at that time the king "met a violent, but ritual end". Ascent to the throne must, therefore, have entailed tacit acceptance of this role as sacrificial offering on behalf of his people. Whatever may have been the case later, it is certain that when Druidism was at its prime, the high festivals were occasions of celebration in which the victim joined and was often the envied focus of all eyes, like the May Queens, themselves probably the descendants of sacrificial victims.

How, conceivably, are such attitudes, running counter to all our feelings of self-preservation and respect for life, to be explained?

Even to begin to understand the notion of human sacrifice we have to keep in mind the three basic paradigms of the societies which practised it. The first of these is that belief in their own crucial proximity to the numen, and the consequent obligations on behalf of mankind at large which this laid upon them.

In the great, endless struggle between order and chaos, theirs is the front-line position.

There are, as in all protracted struggles, the moments of special crisis. For the Aztecs one occurred every fifty-two years. This was the term of their solar 'century'. When the sun set on its last day who knew if it would ever rise again, for all that it might be offered its nourishment of human blood?

Soustelle describes the gathering of anxious crowds up the slopes of the sacred mountain, Uixachtecatl; the astronomer-priests scanning the skies, fearful of the moment when the stars themselves might stop in their courses and gutter out, as the hideous monsters of the end of the world swarmed from their lairs. Minutes then seconds slid by, until, on a precise signal, a victim would be thrown on the altar-slab and his chest ripped open. The fire-stick would be spun in the wound and as it took flame all would know, with indescribable relief, that life was to go on—the world had once more escaped. But for all the joy of that moment, Soustelle comments, "how heavy and blood-drenched a task it was for the priests and the warriors and the emperors, century after century to repel the unceasing onslaughts of the void".

The description could, with very little alteration, be applied to the Celts. Their ages, so Pliny informs us, lasted thirty years and there were, besides, such events as eclipses for which the Druids kept unsleeping vigilance, while Aristotle mentions a custom in which the Celts took up arms to march, not against any mortal enemy, but against the sea, a practice whose origins must lie in some myth of destruction by water, which may itself be associated with the drowning sacrifices.

But it was not only on these rarer and more spectacular occasions that the meticulous performance of ritual secured the salvation of human-kind. No less vital, if less uncommon, were the seasonal ones, those having their base in the primal myth of almost every agricultural society wherein a young god is either abducted or voluntarily descends into the underworld, there to fight some great battle against a malevolent enemy, and by his victory bring the gift of growing corn.

So we find the times of sacrifice coinciding with the high points of the farming year. The goddess Carman, who had a festival in her honour in some parts of Ireland, appears to have been an embodiment of the feminine principle of destructiveness, perhaps akin to the Hindu Shiva. She has three sons whose names mean Violent, Black and Evil, and to encompass the destruction of the *Tuatha De Danann*, she and her offspring blight their corn.

The story is taken up in Manx legend wherein Lugh struggles with Crom Dubh, who, since Dubh means "Black", is obviously one of the sons. It is the victory of Lugh, therefore, which is celebrated in August at the time of the corn-harvest. (According to the Irish version, Carman's three sons are driven across the sea, while Carman is kept as hostage. Either because of humiliation at finding herself a prisoner or overcome by grief at the separation from her sons, she dies. The annual fair in her honour took place near her supposed grave.)

Equally important were the pastoral festivals: Imbolc, marking the lactation of the ewes; Beltain, marking not only the beginning of summer, but also the time when the cattle were driven to their open-air pastures. Or those, like Samain, "summer's end", marking that period of immense peril when the sun begins to lose its power.

There were undoubtedly others—the summer and winter solstices cannot have gone unmarked, as we have already seen. The Irish *Bron Trograin* is referred to, fleetingly, in the *Cattle Raid* as occurring at "earth's sorrowing autumn". It appears to have been an occasion when cattle were sacrificed.

Others must have been purely local. Also a captive-goddess like Carman, Tea was patroness of an annual assembly held at Tara, one of Ireland's most important centres, and a feast was dedicated to a third, Tlachtga.

Outside the festivals, sacrifice must have been offered on other important occasions. It certainly formed part of the ritual by which the king was confirmed in office. From what Caesar tells us, we can assume that royal illness would have led to the offering of propitiatory substitutes. There would have been the times of drought and famine, too, or when pestilence struck humans or livestock. Before any major activity was embarked upon, not only is it likely that auspices would have been taken by the effusion of human blood, but also that sacrifice was offered to guarantee a successful outcome.

The second of the paradigms in which societies like that of the Celts operated was, of course, their view of mythical events. The festivals were neither a commemoration nor a re-enactment of them; they were the events themselves, just as the Catholic church teaches that every "sacrifice" of the Catholic Mass is Christ's actual passion.

And they involved the same dramatis personae: the victim, human or animal, is the actual god. This fact, all other considerations apart, makes the destruction of the physical creature inevitable. Raised above the dross of its kind, it can never return to it. As the bread and wine of the

Communion are the body and blood, so the mare in the ritual described by Gerald of Wales is Macha, the horse-goddess; the mating of king and beast, the actual consummation of the marriage of human and divinity; the eating of the stewed horse-flesh, the absorption of the very godhead. It is, no doubt, because earlier ages were more clearly attuned to such concepts than we are that doctrines like that of transubstantiation were more easily accommodated to their reasoning processes or were introduced in the first place. And it was just this which made the prohibition on the attendance at sacrifice so dreaded a punishment.

CHAPTER ELEVEN

Frenzy, Ecstasy and Possession

IMPOSSIBLE as it is to put ourselves into the minds of those whose bases of reasoning are so far removed from our own, we can still see that the conviction that he was participating in actual events, themselves essential for the very sustenance of life, must have gone a long way towards securing the complicity of the victim, that most astonishing aspect of human sacrifice in its purest form.

But the third of the paradigms I mentioned is one which ensures not just his complicity, but his willing and even enthusiastic acquiescence. This is the victim's own conviction that he has become the incarnation of the godhead itself. Druidism was what is now called a "possession-cult". This, indeed, is the *conditio sine qua non* of all shamanistic systems.[1] The shaman's gods are always accessible, reached as Powell says specifically of the Druids, by trance, vision and ecstasy.

All three are to be found going down to the deepest levels of human experience. One can confidently assert that they are the explanation of

---

[1] Eliade, in *Le Chamanisme et les Techniques Archäiques de l'Extase*, regards, I know, not possession, but the journey he makes into the Other World as characterizing the shaman. This seems to me too restrictive a definition and in any case it is only through his ability to project his spirit or allow himself to be taken over that such journeys are possible.

all those multitudinous cases in religious history in which a deity is treated as though having direct contact with men.

Ecstasy, which means literally "to leave the body", is an almost exact synonym for what contemporary shamans call "spirit flight". It is by its means that they are able to leave their corporeal dwelling-place to venture into the Other World itself (or, when necessary, to travel great distances in the physical world). During such journeys, the body is, in the graphic phrase of the Yaruro Indians of Venezuela, a mere husk, an empty presence. We know it to have a long history. In the 7th Century BC, the Greek Aristeas of Proconnesus, after visiting a distant northerly people, whose religious leaders were patently shamans, brought back with him the gift of "spirit flight" and "bilocation", that is, of leaving his body in one place while he travelled in spirit. The technique may well have been known to and practised by Pythagoras.

The revelatory vision goes back as far as mankind itself. It occurs regularly in Biblical contexts and is always regarded as a way in which the divine will manifests itself. Possibly the best known example in Christianity is the vision of St. John at Patmos which forms the body of the book of *Revelation*, while the teachings of Islam are very largely based on the vision of Mahomet.

The Greeks believed that dreams "descended from Zeus" so that Achilles, when his army was struck by an epidemic before Troy, suggested seeking guidance through them. It was in a dream, too, that Athene, goddess of wisdom, reproved the beautiful Nausicaa for not doing her laundry. When, in obedience to the vision, she took her clothes to the washing-pool next day, she there encountered Odysseus and fell in love, an outcome which Homer leads us to believe was fully intended by the goddess.

The Druids used both vision and "spirit flight". In at least two of the stories of the Druid, Mac Roth, we have examples of it. In one we are told how, having donned his bull's skin cloak and bird headdress, he rose up "in company with the fire, into the air and heavens". Similarly, in another episode he is dispatched by King Ailill, Queen Medb and her love, Fergus, to scan the plain on which the armies of Ulster are mustering. From the ensuing context it is obvious that he must have hovered invisibly over it, for his report covers too vast an area and is too minutely detailed possibly to be accounted for by normal methods of observation, even assuming that, as a known member of the enemy's camp, he would have been allowed to approach so close.

And if we want an example of the use of dream-revelation, we need look no further than the *Tarbfeis* or "bull-dream" in which the identity of the new king is made known.

But it is trance which is most important of all, for it is in this state that the shaman becomes possessed. We know, too, how widespread and venerable the belief was. Two of Moses's associates are spoken of in the *Book of Numbers* as "falling into prophetic ecstasies". The classical writers tell us of the trances which overtook the priestess who served as mouth-piece of the Delphic Oracle, of her groans and shrieks and writhings on her tripod seat, so disconcerting to those who went to consult her. In Tibet, until the Chinese occupation, matters of high state policy were settled by similar consultations, here with a nineteen-year-old Buddhist monk as oracle. Heinrich Harrer in *Seven Years in Tibet* describes the scene as he witnessed it: the trembling that seized the young medium, the tossing head, the eyes "starting from their sockets", the angry red patches which disfigured the face.

If trance is, among other things, the means whereby the shaman is able to seek divine answers to his questions, it is also, together with vision and ecstasy, his means of "managing" the deities, of discovering what must be done in order to secure what is desired for himself, for his client or for his community. At the same time, he, and all who share in the ability of being possessed, take on the powers of the god involved.

Is it, perhaps, belief in possession which lies at the heart of the habit among Celtic warriors of going into battle naked, as witnessed by Polybius at the Battle of Telamon and illustrated on the Pergamene sculptures as well as on Roman coins? It is sufficiently well established to occur even in myth, for in one of the stories of the Cu Chulainn cycle we are told of "a man in a chariot, stark naked". The inevitable parallel is with the Norse "berserkers" who stripped themselves of armour in battle and of whom it was actually said by adversaries that they were possessed of an evil spirit. In at least two mythical contexts stress is laid on the "warrior-heat" of Cu Chulainn. In one he has to bathe three times in icy water, bursting the tub the first time, causing the water to boil the second and only at the third immersion becoming cool enough to dress. In another, he melts the snow for a cubit all round him.

Combat engenders heat, and the physical effort involved in the man-to-man encounters of which the battles of the time largely consisted must have been almost unendurable. But it is also engendered by the trance in which possession takes place and the explicit and detailed reference to warrior-heat seems to indicate that something more than a normal experience is here intended.

The notion that in battle the hero becomes the dwelling-place of a war-god dovetails well with other information, for example, the fact that the Celtic gods are described as leaders of expeditions. Combat is one of those strange experiences in which for its duration a man is hardly himself. He may well be conscious of fear in anticipation, but once in the fray he becomes, as one might say, possessed, often impervious even to serious wounds.

Nakedness in battle, like the berserkers throwing off their armour, might well be a sign for the enemy to see that here was no mortal warrior, but one possessed by the war-god himself. This seems to fit with the long and complex pre-battle rituals in which the Celts indulged.

But there were other occasions when the gods might take up their dwelling with anyone, as for instance during the great communal festivals. We know this occurs in, for instance, the rituals of the Haitian and West African Voodoos, the Brazilian Candomblé communities, the Ethiopian Macha Galla or the Rhodesian Shona. Maya Deren, an American anthropologist who visited Haiti in 1949 to study its dancing, describes how she attended a Voodoo cult meeting and was "possessed" by the love-goddess, Erszulie.

There are even instances of its manifestation in religions as orthodox as Islam and Christianity. Such groups as the snake-handlers of the American "Bible Belt" or the "Shakers" and "Holy Rollers" of the late 18th and early 19th Centuries, as well as the original Quakers, are all, in their way possession-cults. They are distinguished from others only in that, with them, it is the Holy Spirit which takes possession, often heralding its arrival by imparting the "Gift of Tongues" after the manner described in the Acts of the Apostles.

The way in which possession is induced is curiously similar in almost every one of the cults, in essence involving the exposure of the participants to intense and protracted stimulation of the physical senses to the accompaniment of considerable emotional stress.

Typically the setting will be forest or jungle clearing or some equally remote location, as we find favoured by the Voodoos and Candomblés today. Night is usually the chosen time.

Far from the comforting security of home, surrounded by the potent sounds and smells of nature at night, the scene lit only by the flickering of cressets or fires, the participants feel themselves bound together in a mysterious union of which one of the strongest factors must be the working of the herd instinct always active in times of common stress.

Preliminaries may include the slaughter of an animal and the sprinkling of its blood upon them and they are further involved in what is happening through endless, litany-like chants to which they give the responses.

Often stimulants will be used, either drugs or alcohol, for both were (and still are) regarded as producing states of mind which approximate to the divine. To qualify as a Brahmin, for example, a man had to prove he came of a line of *soma*-takers. The name, *soma*, given to the latex extracted from certain plants, now unknown, but whose effect was probably much like the modern LSD, was also the name of the Vedic moon-goddess, thus linking her with its effects. In Scandinavia, drunkenness was regarded as a holy state and poetry itself was the "Precious Mead".

(This view was largely shared by the Zoroastrians of Persia.)

Perhaps most vital of all elements was the constant rhythmical music and drumming which accompanied the entire proceedings. Maya Deren has given us a first-hand description of the effect upon her: how gradually foot-tapping gave place to bodily spasms which themselves gradually became spontaneous and uncontrollable like a tic, until at last the sound seemed to take over, charging her whole body to the point where she felt as if it would burst her skin. In less intense form, most people who have been to jazz or "pop" concerts can record similar experiences, with some members of the audience so carried away they leap to their feet, clapping, dancing and shouting as if they had become one with the pulse of the music.

But can we assume Druidism to have been a possession-cult of this kind? The evidence seems to me to tend unmistakably in that direction. In many of the customs whose beginnings we can trace to Druidism we find night, fires and dancing—often described by witnesses as "Bacchanalian"—as essential elements. We have the practice of rites in isolated locations. We know the Druids to have used drums and they are also found in folk-festivals in both Man and Jersey. In the former, a skin-drum called a "dollan" was used and horns were blown throughout the night of May Eve. In Jersey a drum, was improvised from a wash-boiler.

Myths of divine intoxications are so common and similar among the Indo-European peoples that a single source must be supposed. This alone would indicate that the Celts probably shared in the beliefs and practices, using mead for rituals. As additional evidence, there is the divine queen, Medb, whose name itself derives from "mead" and who is also called the "Drunk Woman" and "the Drunk-Making Woman". In one legend, we are told how the hero, Finn, got a drink of "precious water" from one of the daughters of Bec mac Buain, while he and two of his companions were visiting Other World beings in a *sidh*. A poem by an anonymous author in the Mivirian Archaeology of Wales, a collection of documents of the early Middle Ages, speaks of a nocturnal religious feast to mark the summer equinox at which mead and wine were distributed.

There is also analogical evidence that Druidism was a possession-cult. Besides being the essential distinguishing mark of shamanistic systems, it is to be found in most societies practising human sacrifice in so far as we know about them. It is quite plain that the long rituals of the Aztec feasts in which all took part and which, incidentally, were one of the rare occasions when it was permissible to use intoxicants, were directed towards inducing the precise kind of state Maya Deren describes. Here, too, chanting, rhythmic drumming and dancing—often lasting for days and nights on end—were important constituents.

The mood of increased suggestibility, to use the jargon of psychology, which can lead to such states of exultation has, of course, been the subject of an extensive literature, going back, indeed, to the rites of both Dionysus and the Pythian Apollo, both involving possession.

In his book, *Battle for the Mind*, the British psychiatrist William Sargant has made a close study of such phenomena. He shows how the saturation of the individual by sensual stimuli, under conditions in which there is emotional stress, can lead to dissociation and disorientation.

One effect of long exposure is what he calls "reversion of the faculties": food previously repugnant becomes appetizing; what was once pleasurable loses its fascination, and what had been avoided becomes desirable. All these can be seen in the manifestation of the possession-cults as we observe them today and it becomes understandable how, taking part in them, normal people will, for example, lick avidly at the welling blood of a freshly beheaded cockerel.

It can be argued, obviously, that none of the possession cults as we now know them today actually practices human sacrifice and that this must introduce an element they lack which could radically alter the reactions of the participants.

While this is true, we do, however, have a corpus of information from situations in which people are subjected to the presence or fear of death over long periods. We know, for example, of the disorientation produced in those who underwent constant bombing during the Blitz, or which has been found by army and air force psychiatrists among men exposed to combat for protracted periods. Typically, the "reversion of the faculties" is such that a minor stimulus will cause a quite disproportionate reaction. A raised voice will cause a helpless flood of tears, as bewildering to the victim as to the speaker; a tiny joke inspires paroxysmal laughter, bordering on and perhaps overspilling into hysteria. By contrast, that normally shunned is embraced, including death itself. Front-line soldiers will suddenly leave their fox-holes and run into the enemy's machine-guns. And, as Sargant makes clear, it is people who normally most enjoy life who will be most overwhelmed by the desire to die—an illuminating insight into the Celts and their sacrificial practices.

The leaders of the Mau Mau revolt of the fifties among the Kikuyu people of Kenya used every means at their disposal to give their organization and its activities a religious cast and to make recruits feel like converts. This included ceremonies of initiation deliberately designed to evoke excited horror and whose details are such it has never been thought proper to publish them. Among Mau Mau terrorists moved into the "Death Rows" of gaols just before execution, singing and laughter were constant, as though the inmates were guests at some hilarious party.

Silas Tood was among the converts of John Wesley whose emotional style of preaching was such it could drive penitents to roll on the ground like epileptics in the belief they had been seized with the Holy Spirit. After conversion he made it his duty to visit the condemned in Newgate Prison, where he prevailed on the turnkeys to allow these unfortunates to congregate in one cell for a religious service, which included public confession and a moving sermon. The rest of the night would pass, as he relates, in praying, hymn-signing and rejoicing, "the Lord God Himself being evidently in the midst of them".

This elevated mood lasted to the moment of death. On the journey by open cart to Tyburn, one woman, Mary Pinner, "continued ... singing, praising and giving glory to God without intermission till she arrived at the gallows"—shades of the women-victims of the Aztec corn-god. Even in her last moments she sought to hearten her fellow-sufferers.

And if any doubts about the anaesthetizing effect of these religious frenzies linger we have some convincing pieces of evidence. In some of the cults, observed by modern anthropologists, drastic self-chastisement is practised at the climax of celebrations. This can take the form of participants lashing themselves with thongs so that the flesh is visibly lacerated with every stroke. They give every impression of being totally impervious to the pain they are inflicting on themselves.

We know that during the festival of the Phrygian Cybele, a possession cult if ever there was one, some of the young males reached the point at which, in imitation of the goddess's eunuch-priests, they castrated themselves on the spot and laughingly hurled their bleeding genitals through the first open window they saw. (The recipients regarded them as in the nature of a good luck talisman.) In some of the rites of Astarte, a deity possibly related to the Celtic Adraste invoked by Boudicca, a sword was placed in readiness for such self-dismemberment.

There is, as it happens, another possible link between Druidism and known possession-cults, one which also links them with Britain and so gives support to Caesar's statement that it was here that Druidism began.

His list of Gaulish gods bears witness to the importance placed on the deity he designates as Apollo, and this is amply borne out by the archaeological evidence of invocations extending right across the Celtic world.

The Gaulish Apollo was, of course, Belenos the Brilliant, like his counterpart associated with the sun. But the equivalence actually goes much deeper: Belenos or Beli and Apollo both derive their names from a single Indo-European root-word, that which gives us "apple" in English, *Apfel* in German and *Aval* in Celtic. This last form is found in

Avalon, the island to which the wounded Arthur was conveyed by his sister, Morgan le Fay. But the word also occurs in three other islands: Avallach, Emain Ablach and the Isle of Abalum. The inclusion of the *apple*-element in these three names is obviously significant. One of the reasons is that, like Avalon, they are all "Isles of the Blessed". Here summer is perpetual and, so the fruits of summer can be plucked throughout the year. (One is powerfully reminded of the Garden of Eden which, like so much else in the Bible, shows traces of shamanism.)

But the other reason may connect them with Apollo. The Isle of Abalum takes us far out of what is usually thought of as Celtic territory and up to the Baltic, to the region where amber, otherwise "the tears of Apollo", is to be found. Tacitus describes it as a place in which "the last radiance of the setting sun can linger until dawn". The credulous locals, he informs us, believed they could hear the sound "he (i.e. the sun) makes as he rises from the waves and can see the shape of his horses and the rays on his head". Here, then, is an image of Apollo, driving the sun-chariot, exactly as we have him represented in Greek myth. A head with sun-rays emerging from it is a well-known way of representing him, and is found not only in Graeco-Roman connexions, but also in Celtic ones as in the Medusa-head found at Bath. This last shows Belenos/Apollo in the guises of both sun god and god of healing, as he is repeatedly found in Celtic custom.

Pre-historic representations of a sun-chariot have been found in northern Denmark.

All this lends support to the view now gaining ground that the cult of Apollo, once regarded as quintessentially Greek and, therefore, of Mediterranean provenance, may actually be northern. This coincides with the Greeks' own stated belief that for three months each year the god lived among a northerly people whose land was "beyond the North Wind". Their mythology makes him the offspring of Zeus and Leto, who is herself the daughter of the Titans—in other words, giants, like both the Celts and their gods. Apollo has a sister, none other than Diana or Artemis, the successor, as we saw, of a long line of moon/fertility goddesses, possibly related to the Celtic pantheon through Dana or Ana, founder of the *Tuatha De Danann*. Thus, on the internal evidence of mythologies Greek and Celtic, we are among very ancient divinities and it is generally held that Apollo was an interloper on the Greek Olympus: an importation for whom their myths had to be adapted to accord him a place.

In any case, the ecstatic nature of his cult and that of Diana/Artemis is completely at odds with those of other Greek deities. His most famous shrine was, of course, that at Delphi, where he was worshipped as the Pythian Apollo on account of his slaughter of the snakes there. It was, as we have already seen, the object of a Celtic expedition in 270 BC, and

Markale suggests that this was religiously motivated. Delphi itself is situated in a landscape of cliffs, ravines and running streams welling up from subterranean sources. With this added to its religious reputation it must have been exactly the sort of place to fascinate the Celts. It claimed also to be the centre of the world—the omphallos or navel—and the precise point of this was marked by a stone. Centres, too, were of deep significance to Celtic religion.

We know that there was a continuing interest in the Greek Apollo among northerly peoples because there is a description of an annual offering sent to his temple at Delos by an unidentifiable northern people. They are, in fact, the almost legendary "Hyperboreans", the name meaning more or less literally "People from Beyond the North Wind", and they were the race from whom the Greek Aristeas learnt the art of "spirit flight".

But who were they? And were they actually a single race?

Much research has been expended on their identification and they have variously been declared to be Balts, Eskimos and Scandinavians, as well as the inhabitants of the apocryphal Atlantis. Piggott most persuasively suggests that they may even have been the Chinese, while Markale asks: "Are they the *Tuatha De Danann?*" My own conjecture is that the name was simply one applied to the peoples of any northerly *terra incognita*, in much the same way as "Moors" was applied to virtually anyone with a dark skin up almost to the 18th Century.

There is, however, general agreement that in one passage from Hecateus (circa 500 BC), quoted by Diodorus, the land of the Hyperboreans can only be Britain. The author describes a country not smaller than Sicily, lying opposite Gaul, of which Hyperboreans are the inhabitants. Hecateus is not given to reporting rumour. He was a painstaking and judicious writer who had himself travelled extensively and described his observations in his *Circuit of the Earth* which, like so many books of the ancient world, has been lost to us and is known only in quotation.

The island of the Hyperboreans was, he tells us, the birthplace of Leto—that daughter of giants—and on this account her son, Apollo, was venerated there above all the gods. He tells us additionally that the island housed a vast temple in circular form, which can only be Stonehenge, and the passage goes on to describe the system of calendration there used which is based on a nineteen-year cycle. At the end of each of these periods, Apollo was said to visit the island, playing the harp to accompany the dancing of his worshippers in revelry which apparently lasted for several days.

The Greek god is, as we know, credited with giving mankind the harp, which he had himself received from the hands of Hermes (or Mercury), and this has become a uniquely Celtic instrument, found in both Wales and Ireland.

Druidic time-computation with its basis of solar and lunar cycles must also have involved the veneration of their presiding deities. We can only conjecture at the identity of their moon-goddess (?*Dana*); but we know that Belenos was the sun-god. The period of nineteen-years which it requires for lunar and solar years to achieve synchronicity is also, as it happens, the period between eclipses. These were events of the most enormous magnitude, arousing an intense and understandable awe. The prediction of eclipses must, therefore, have formed one of the most important applications of Stonehenge—a point made by Professor Hawkins.[2]

The reference to music and dancing in Hecateus's description brings to mind the techniques of inducing possession. And what is more likely, since during an eclipse the sun-god was observably absent from his normal tasks, than that he should have taken up his abode among his worshippers? This surely is the sense in which the notion of a visit to earth by the sun-god would be understood.

Whether Hecateus is referring to the Druids or their predecessors, the priesthood of the people who built the megaliths, here we have him showing his special favour to mortals devoted to his cult.

Perhaps one final witness ought to be heard in this argument that Druidism was a shamanistic possession cult. He is S M Shirokogoroff, who wrote his study of shamanism, based on first hand observation, under the title *Psychomental Complex of the Tungus* in 1935.

In it he describes a festival among the Tungus shamans. It begins with the shaman himself chanting, then dancing and slowly involving all the participants in his actions as they repeat the refrains. As the tempo increases the shaman himself becomes possessed, but his possession is felt by everyone present so that "the state of many participants is now near to that of the shaman himself". A state of mass ecstasy supervenes in which hallucinations and mass acts take place. Sensing his audience is with him the shaman becomes still more active and this, too, is passed back to them. The passage pulsates with the feeling of Druidism.

In Shirokogoroff's description the frenzied spiral continues to ascend until something like exhaustion takes over, but we can well envisage a totally different climax: one which a central figure in the proceedings, writhing and entranced convinced he is the incarnation of the god, goes joyously, remorselessly to his bloody death.

[2]Intriguingly, the old name for Salisbury, on whose plain Stonehenge is located, Sarum, is an obvious latinization of an earlier name. *Saros* was the Babylonic word for 3600, the number of days between eclipses, still recalled in the "Saros-cycle" used by astronomers.

Nonetheless the precise thing which made human-sacrifice possible may, in the end, lead to its decline.

Ronald Knox's book *Enthusiasm* is largely preoccupied with those emotional and fundamentalist Christian sects of which Wesley's was an example, but which were themselves merely latterday revivals of possession-cults, a fact hard to absorb when one considers the respectability and orthodoxy of modern Methodism.

"Always," he reminds us, "the first fervours evaporate; prophecy dies out, and the charismatic is merged in the institutional." One cannot believe other than that this was true of late Druidism. Lacking the old exultation, human sacrifice became a mere part of magical liturgy with none, least of all the screaming victims, recalling what once it had represented. No doubt under these circumstances it was doomed to extinction, a process which, as we have seen, may have already been occurring.

CHAPTER TWELVE

A Time of Decline

IN that tour de force of Celtic scholarship, *Pagan Celtic Britain*, Professor Anne Ross expresses the view that in the period up to the time of their extinction by the Romans the Druids were actively promoting a single group of gods as a step towards national unity—the mirage which both bewitched and eluded the Celts throughout their history. Among those she nominates for membership of this select band are Taranis, Esus, Teutatis, Lugh and Cernunnos.

The view I have myself put forward is, of course, almost diametrically the opposite one: namely the gods like Taranis, Esus, Teutatis and Cernunnos, representative of an original strain of deities going back into Celtic pre-history were actually undergoing displacement by the later strain of the *Tuatha De Danann*. One indication of this is the relatively minor role played by the earlier gods in the myths—and whatever may have happened to these, we must certainly suppose that the form in which they have reached us had developed from the last fully pagan versions so that they would to some extent reflect the situation as it was at that time.

The argument that the Druids were engaged in bringing about Celtic national unity is not, of course, a new one, but it has the inestimable benefit of providing a ready and apparently plausible answer to the question of why the Romans decided to invade and subjugate Gaul when they did. Having twice suffered at Celtic hands, the argument runs, the thought that these menacing neighbours might achieve political unity was too much for Roman apprehensions. Caesar was dispatched to put a stop to them once and for all.

And if a move towards unity was in train, there was only one body in Celtic society capable of advancing it. This was the Druids, not only more powerful than the chiefs themselves, but also through their own organization, capable of traversing the tribal bounds and so of resolving internal jealousies. The most natural way of bringing their objective about would be through promoting the worship of a single pantheon of unarguably "Druidic" gods who, though they might not supplant them, would at least take precedence over the tribal ones. This would represent the ideological unification which is always the precondition to political unity.

The view has undergone considerable criticism, however, and in this case one finds it difficult not to side with the critics.

First, there is no real evidence that the invasion of Gaul was, as it were, the result of a national decision by the Romans. Caesar, for whom at that time becoming emperor can have been no more than an idle dream, was simply using his consular powers to intervene in a quarrel between two Gaulish tribes, one of which, the Aedui, was under Rome's protection. At the same time, of course, he might well acquire for himself some military glory. There is absolutely nothing in the preceding events which makes it look as if Celtic nationalism was astir, let alone a process of unification in train; on the contrary, there is every appearance that the quarrel between the Aedui and Helvetii was yet another in the incessant cycle of inter-tribal conflicts.

The legend of Druidic power rests very largely on Caesar's own account of them and it was in his interest to make the menace of the Gauls appear as great as possible so as to magnify his own achievement. But, as he has pointed out, his main source of information was probably Posidonius, who had written at least some decades earlier and the state of affairs he was describing may well have changed. In fact, if we turn to Strabo we find him categorically stating that one of the most impressive of the Druids' political powers, that of intervening to stop intertribal wars, belonged to the past.

If the Celts really were already moving towards national unification one can scarcely conceive anything more likely to give it extra stimulus than foreign invasion. The need for a single front against the common enemy was so obvious it would surely have persuaded the last waverers to sink their tribal differences. Far from this happening, all the evidence is that the Celtic tribes behaved as they always had. Internecine and dynastic struggles continued under Roman noses, inviting and often receiving their attention and intervention.

There was no improvement later when Vercingetorix represented the one last chance the Gauls had of winning back complete liberty. The Avernian leader failed in the end, because he could not find a sufficient number of tribal leaders ready to resolve or forget their individual disagreements for the emergency and throw their weight in with him. There is no sign that the Druids were advocating support for Vercingetorix. Or that if they were, anyone heeded them.

This is not, of course, to say that religion is not capable of providing a rallying point for movements of national unification. One thinks of Mahomet and Islam. But what we have here is what is in effect a new religion which gives nationalism the aura of a divine mission. At least, if it was to provide a unifying force the religion must be in the full flood of its power.

The indications are that Celtic life was undergoing a process of secularization of which the replacement of the chiefs in Gaul by a magistracy—the *vergobrets*—elected for a year, looks like a part. It is hard to see this, as some have, as a step in the Druidic plan to build a Celtic nation. The *vergobrets* came from the class of knights, in other words the laity, and while a "magistrate" in Roman terms fulfilled rather more comprehensive functions than we should expect of one today, these certainly included the administration of law. Hitherto, this had been an entirely Druidic prerogative, so that their role had effectively been diminished.

This is paralleled by diminution in other spheres.

We do not know when the practice of sacrificing kings had ceased, but even in Ireland, with its strongly conservative tradition, it seemed to have been in abeyance for some time. In other words, the Druids no longer held untrammelled power even over the lives of sovereigns.

By the time of the Claudian invasion of Britain we have in the conduct of Cartimandua what must have been open defiance of Druidic counsel. For they can hardly have been anything but opposed to her actions in handing over her own husband's birthright to Roman "protection" without a show of resistance. Roman occupation could only lead to the persecution of the Druids and this in a tribal territory in which they had once enjoyed unrivalled power.

It seems to me that we may have in all this the outline of an answer to a riddle.

Those invaders who founded the first great Indo-European civilization, that of the Hittites, round the Black Sea coast, undoubtedly took their shamans with them. But as they abandoned their former nomadic life in favour of a settled one centred on farm and town, as invariably happens, first chieftains, then kings, took on the sacerdotal role and the power of the shamans dwindled until at the height of the empire they were little more than "wise men" or "wise women" consulted by individuals who believed that some adversity was caused by the visitation of malign "spirits".

What happened with the Hittites is typical. It happened, not only in other Indo-European societies, such as Rome and Greece, but also in Egypt. In all these, as in most other cases, the role of mediator between gods and people was taken over by the secular head of state. King-as-mediator was so much the accepted pattern that some earlier scholars questioned whether the Druids could be an Indo-European manifestation at all and were not, in fact, an importation. This was before it had come to be realized that Brahminism was also Indo-European in origin, so that we now have not one but two bodies of clearly shamansitic lineage which displayed this ability to survive where other shamans were displaced.

Kendrick suggests the answer lies in the fact that Druids had taken command of education and so were able to perpetuate their doctrines, but this seems to me to raise as many questions as it answers. The Celtic aristocracy which patronized the Druidic schools would have done so only if they found what was being taught in them desirable. They have several alternatives: they could leave their young untaught or restrict their education to what would be imparted to them by their foster-parents. Or, like the Romans, they could have employed teachers from abroad, notably from Greece, with whom they had many links. So Druidic schools would not automatically have ensured the perpetuation of Druidism; they would have done so only in so far as the ideologies of religion and society were in accord—as on the whole they were.

Objections can be raised to most of the other attempts to provide an answer to this question of Druidic survival.

It is, as one might expect, a complex one, though I believe the real answer to contain two strands: as one could express it, a truth and an inference.

The truth is that there was plainly something about the Druids which deeply impressed their classical observers (and these may well have included minds as keen as those of Aristotle and Pythagoras). They were led to put them on equal terms with those two most remarkable bodies of the Ancient World, the Babylonian priesthood and the Persian Magi. No one, aware of the facts, could fail to realize that these two bodies with the Brahmins—who are still, more or less, with us—made an enormous contribution to human development. This very real and demonstrable knowledge, which the Druids possessed in at least some measure, is what distinguishes them from other shamans. It was something of a quite different order from crudely "analogic" treatments used by, say, a Hittite witch who "cured" sexual impotence, for example, by dressing the patient in black clothes and then taking them off again with spells. (Though, of course, we must not overlook the fact that the Druids may well have used such methods, too.) To a greater or lesser extent, Druidic skills "worked"—were real. And this ensured that they could not simply be pushed aside. In order to bring about their complete displacement the church itself had to take over many of their functions—those of teaching, of medicine, of astronomy, for instance.

The inference I mentioned is that the Druids were supposedly cut down in their prime and, had they not been, they, like the Brahmins, might still have been with us.

This seems to me a misreading of the evidence. The importance of their role might have prolonged the Druids' existence; it could not ensure immortality in the face of other threats. The process which had taken place in Hittite, Greek, Roman and other civilizations so much earlier was the playing out of an ancient drama: that between the needs of the individual—or family—and the sometimes conflicting one of society at large. In his basic form, the shaman is mediator between the forces of the supernatural and the individual, at most the single unit of hunters, fishermen or stockbreeders. Through the introduction of the totem-spirit this mediation begins to take on a communal character and this "socialization" process continues to an inevitable end. With the Hittites, the Greeks and the Romans we have religion becoming one with the state; the state, as exemplified by its ruling class, has the sanction of religion for its acts. Its demands, not those of the individual, are paramount. Naturally, this circumscribes freedom and independence and, especially in times of repression, sends people looking back nostalgically to the times when no such restrictions existed.

If we can detect a moment at which such change begins, it surely must be that at which urbanization begins and "the city" in the true sense—as a machine for living in—emerges as centre. This with its communalized services brings men into a real interdependence with each other, a truly institutionalized life begins. But there is a practical point involved, too: the concentration of population into a smaller area means they will expect to conduct worship within that area; they will no longer be prepared to make pilgrimages into the heart of the countryside. They are now the centre; formerly it was the religious sanctuary, the *nemeton*, drawing families to worship in it from over a wide area.

This change had long since occurred in Persian or Hittite history. Nowhere is this better demonstrated than in their artistic activity. The Celts did not always portray the world naturalistically, but they caught its feeling as first-hand observers. The twisting, convolute shapes they impart to plants which may not themselves be recognizable as any known species have, nonetheless, the air of real plants. They would not surprise us if we came across them growing. With the Persians, the Hittites or the Babylonians nature has become stylized, urbanized one might say. Winged lions, marching warriors, robed kings are constructed from the forms of geometry not nature. They have become, in fact, mere decoration for architecture, particularly the grandiose architecture of cities.

There is, however, some evidence to suggest that towns, often built on locations associated with their deities, were becoming increasingly important to the Celts as well.

And it is in this revolutionary change to urban centres that the shaman is likely to be swamped. He may well be banished altogether, as happened in Rome. But if he is to survive it is by the surrender of a large measure of his power and independence of action, so that he comes nearer to being the seer- or astrologer-royal. This must have happened in Egypt; to some extent it also happened to the Magi and the Babylonian priesthoods. Not even the Brahmins were totally exempt from it.

Was this also happening to the Druids? Certainly, from the Roman conquest on whenever one comes upon an individual or a group who look like successors to the Druids two things are striking: that they are largely dependent on royal patronage and that religion has now passed into other hands. The magicians of Vortigern illustrate the one; Merlin the other. By the times of the Arthurian legends as we have received them, the religion is Christianity, its representatives the bishops, priests, nuns and monks who figure in the stories. Merlin is no more than a magician, a very powerful one to be sure, but quite divorced from any fully religious activity.

I do not believe that religion is the mere reflection of socio-economic circumstances—there are too many cases where the religion has antedated, sometimes by centuries, a particular set of circumstances.

The two are, nonetheless, interconnected. The Catholic Church of the Middle Ages was at once mirror and complement to feudalism; the European Reformist movements coincided with the Renaissance and the rise of humanism. The great victories of Christian evangelism corresponded with the Industrial Revolution and the rise of laissez-faire capitalism.

If, therefore, Brahminism and Druidism are comparable it is because the India of the *rajas* and the Gaul and Britain of the *riges* were comparable—the very words are cognates of an Indo-European radical. Both were tribal, agrarian societies, aristocratic and heroic, with petty monarchs at their heads. Both were dogged by an inherent tendency to inter-tribal dissension. The society discovered by the Muslim invaders of the 10th Century AD must have been very much like that found in Gaul and Britain in the last century BC. One might risk going further and declare that it was very little changed by the time the Europeans began arriving in India in the 16th Century. It was precisely because of constant quarrelling between the *rajas* and their willingness, like the Celts, to accept any alliance of the moment, even with a foreign invader, and, without consideration of its long-term results, that the British were able to conquer. They did so by using precisely the tactics used by the Romans, that of bringing one ruler after another into cliency; only where this was impossible was military force resorted to. What we can say, therefore, is that Druidism, like Brahminism, provided a relationship with the supernatural appropriate to a certain stage of social development.

The survival of Brahminism is due to a number of factors of which the continuation of Indian society in a largely unaltered state is one, but—though fundamental—only one. We are not, however, concerned with the survival of the Brahmins, but with that of the Druids, who as a bald, brutal fact have departed. Though as I hope to demonstrate, they recur in history and can be traced over a long period, it is in a much changed and reduced state.

We can only speculate about the way in which religious ideas develop. The ascent of the first shaman to the world of spirits no doubt increases the possibility that he will be joined there by others, especially as society itself become more complex and shamanism begins to split and diversify. Each of the newcomers will have unarguably "magical" characteristics, but he will have them in admixture with something else: he will be the physician-shaman who becomes the god of healing; the metal-working shaman who becomes the smith-god; the lawgiver-shaman who duly becomes the god of law and of justice. At the same time, this admission of human to spirit world would probably lead to the gradual "humanizing" of the totemic spirits, beginning with a phase in which animal and human phases alternate or in which zoomorphic qualities are retained—human body and animal head, for instance. So the mare from whose belly all things proceed, becomes the divine woman-horse.

But this very proliferation carries with it its own threat, all the more ominous since it is quite inconceivable that such enormous power as the Druids wielded could possibly have gone totally unchallenged. It is the nature of power, more than anything else to breed envy. The threat implied might have been less if they had been able to keep it inviolate to themselves. Unfortunately, they could not; they had to share it with others. It was they alone, for example, who could impart to the chieftain the charisma necessary for him to rule. They did it, as we know, through his ritual marriage to the territorial goddess. Such practices are well known. In Haiti marriage between a mortal and *loa*, or spirit, are so frequent that printed marriage certificates are available for the purpose.

And marriage, even spiritual marriage, is an intimate relationship. At any rate one might expect the mortal partner could claim he knew more about his spouse and her needs than any outsider. In other words, he is liable to usurp the role of mediator. In Haiti, those married to *loa* themselves often become Voodoo priests. The Celtic chieftain had an added incentive to assume the mediative role: his own life could be at stake.

But jealousy of the Druids with their male exclusiveness could well have reached its apogee among the fiercely independent tribal women. If one judges from the two cases known to history it looks as though this was the case. As Ross remarks, Queen Cartimandua behaves with such high-handedness she seems to regard herself as the incarnation of her own goddess, Brigantia, otherwise Brigid, invoking her with sacrifice. Boudicca behaves similarly with Adraste, not only seeking assistance in bad times, but showing her gratitude for benefits received with monstrously cruel rituals of human sacrifice which seem to be entirely her own invention. She first cut the breasts of her women victims, then stuffed them into their mouths "as though they ate them" and finally impaled them lengthwise on stakes.

What the various sources also show is a growing confusion between religious and secular leadership. Conchobhar was, of course, the son of a Druid, and the uncertainty as to whether Diviciacus was also one could well have arisen from the fact that even if he was not he must have possessed some religious functions. He was certainly chief of the Aedui. The doubts which arise can only mean that the lines of demarcation had become blurred.

The conclusion from all this is that in the years up to the Roman conquest some dilution of Druidic power must have taken place. This accounts for their total absence from Caesar's accounts of his actual campaigns, in contrast with his assertions of their power in Celtic life in the first chapter of his book. These are facts which have struck a number of observers.

We may well suspect, if only on the analogy of Cartimandua and Boudicca, that the territorial, that is to say the tribal, gods invoked by the chieftains or their directly-appointed nominees, were beginning to take precedence over the exclusively Druidic ones. The process by which the shaman was displaced as sole mediator, completed in other societies, was now taking place in the Celtic. Religion was turning into a pure instrument of state under the control of the state's rulers.

This may solve the problem of the *guatuatri*. The one thing about which we can be reasonably sure is that they were nothing to do with the Druids. The chances are, then, that they were a priesthood of exactly the

type with which the classical writers were familiar, and being mere pale
imitations of their own were deemed unworthy of mention.

There is no doubt that Celtic religion, as distinct from Druidism,
continued under Roman auspices. Most of the temple-building took
place in Gallo-Roman times. In several cases these were erected on the
foundations of earlier structures. This resembles the later Christian
practice of placing churches on the sites of former pagan buildings,
sometimes employing in the new structure the materials which had gone
into the earlier ones. We know, in fact, that in their efforts to extirpate
Druidism, the Romans cut down a number of the sacred groves, including that near Massilia, mentioned by Lucan.

Nor is there any doubt that of the representations of deities found by
archaeologists and dated to Gallo-Roman times, the greater majority
were territorial gods. As we know, even the legionaries themselves were
invoking Celtic gods and not always equating them with those of the
Graeco-Roman pantheon.

The one thing the Romans did not provide, however, was a priesthood, an administrative body to replace what they set out to destroy. But
since religion continued with so little apparent disturbance after the
disappearance of the Druids, one can only suppose there was already in
existence one which could take over or had perhaps begun to take over.
And, on balance, one might think that it could well have been quite
ready to help the Romans in their efforts to weaken Druidism.
Traditionalist enclaves where their way would have been followed must
have continued in Britain and Gaul, probably in secret. They possessed,
too, their magical skills for which a demand would have existed then, as
there was a demand for the services of the witches and folk-doctors later.
Indeed, if there is one thing which more than all else demonstrates the
ease with which the supersession of Druidism took place, as well as the
fact that they must have been in decline, it was the speed with which
they were allowed to re-enter Celtic life under the Romans. The conquest of Gaul had been accomplished by the middle of the 1st Century
BC. Less than a hundred years later Pomponious Mela was writing what
sounds like an eye-witness account of their performing token human
sacrifices. This could not have been tolerated if the Druids were still seen
as a potential threat to the occupiers.

We continue, of course, to hear of the Druids, but it is in two main
connexions. One is as the fortune-tellers in the *Historia Augusta*; the other
is Ausonius's mention of Phoebicius as keeper of the temple of Belenos.
But quite obviously by this time the name "Druid" was probably
applied to any priest serving Celtic as opposed to other gods.

CHAPTER THIRTEEN

The Heroic Age: Arthur

I F Britain had, indeed, been the birthplace of Druidism, it was appropriate enough it should have become its sepulchre. Certainly Britain became the refuge of the Gaulish Druids after the Roman conquest and the abortive rebellion of Vercingetorix. Evidence of these refugees is evinced by the presence of pottery styles found in Gaul. Cartimandua herself may have been of Belgian lineage.

The home-in-exile for these religious fugitives was most certainly the all-important centre of Môn or Anglesey. They were not, of course, suffered to continue there for long. The attack on Anglesey, under Suetonius Paulinus, marked the final moves by the Romans in subjugating the major Celtic territories. Ireland, isolated from these events, went on, yet the inevitable impression one receives is that even here the Druids had declined. In so far as the stories of Cu Chulainn cycle are historical, many scholars have suggested that they record events which took place about the time of the life of Christ. In the stories we have Druids functioning as teachers, as physicians, as magic bards when they emerge from the cataract of Es Ruaid to charm the Connaught armies, most of all as prophets. They hardly appear, however, as the governors of a theocracy. Indeed, when the "magical harpers" appear from Es

Ruaid, they are mistaken for Ulster spies and have to turn themselves into deer to escape pursuit.

These were, one could say with truth, twilit days for the Celts. Nevertheless, the days of glory were not quite ended, though now the centre was, indubitably, Britain.

Arthur, once and future king, remains the object of furious controversy. A native Celtic king? A Roman who had either continued to live in Britain after the withdrawal of the legions or had returned, more or less as a soldier of fortune at the same time British were calling for help? A pure fiction with or without a basis in reality? Perhaps an old Celtic god revived?

The historical facts can be set down with confidence. In AD 410, Rome gave notice that internal problems made it impossible for her forces any longer to police Britain and her troops were withdrawn after 360 years of occupation. The people had long been the victims of sudden and bloody descents by Saxon raiders crossing the North Sea and by Picts and Scots from the Northern marches which even the efforts of the Roman troops had been unable to check. With these gone, however, the way was open for ceaseless assault. Within a short time invading Jutes, Angles and Saxons were establishing colonies, while the departure of the patrols along Hadrian's Wall allowed the Picts and Scots to make forays deep into the country.

It was in these circumstances that in AD 443 the British people made their famous appeal to Rome for assistance. Officially, it produced no response, though it is likely that some Romans made the journey, a few possibly out of hope of gain, a few, possibly because as soldiers from the former occupying army they had formed a real affection for Britain and its people. We know it was quite common for patrician mothers to speak of their soldier sons as having "gone to fight in the barbarian armies". In any event, their numbers in Britain were insufficient to turn the tide of invasion in favour of the indigenous population.

Some measure of the boldness of Picts and Scots can be gathered from the fact that their forays were taking them as far south as Kent, where they were driving the Kentish chieftain, Vortigern, to desperation. It was this which led him to make the cardinal error so often made by Celtic leaders. Apparently under the delusion that complete strangers knew, understood and were prepared to abide by the usages of *Celsine* or cliency, he looked for an ally and his eye alighted on the Jutes. The Gaulish Aeduans had made a precisely similar mistake in seeking Roman aid in an inter-tribal quarrel and brought on their people's head total subjection.

From earliest times Vortigern has played the role of historical villain on account of this imprudent act. The Welsh triads describe him as one of "the three drunkards of Britain": his intoxication being not that of

wine but of lust—his infatuation for Ronwen, daughter of Horsa. The
judgment is perhaps a little harsh. It is possible he was helplessly in love,
it is certain that he was an old man, and an extremely conservative one,
deeply inbued with the spirit of times past, and beside himself in trying
to protect his own people.

We know that his appeal succeeded, Hengist and Horsa came to his
aid and succeeded in their immediate objective.

According to the 9th Century Nennius, Horsa fell in the ensuing
battle, but as his compensation Vortigern gave Hengist the Isle of
Thanet. It was not sufficient, and the Jutes became ever more importu-
nate, until the hapless Vortigern realized he was fighting, instead of only
Picts and Scots, the Jutes as well. Too tired for war, he fled westwards
and built himself a citadel in Wales.

It is at this point, that according to Nennius, the first of the major
characters of the Arthurian story makes his entry. Determined to make
his citadel impregnable at all costs, Vortigern consulted his magicians.
They advised him to enlist the benevolence of the gods by sacrificing an
orphan child and burying this body in the foundations. The victim
finally selected was, says Nennius, a little boy called Ambrosius, the
Welsh form of which is 'Emrys', son of a Roman couple of consular rank.

The boy saves himself by displaying a gift for prophecy so spectacular
the king reprieves him. Three centuries after Nennius, Geoffrey of
Monmouth gives substantially the same account, but with one
significant change: the child-victim's name has become Merlin, or in
Welsh "Myrddin".

Why the change? There is another "Myrddin" known to history and
he is the 6th Century Welsh bard of that name. So whatever other
possibilities may be open, it is a historical impossibility for him to have
been involved in a struggle with the Saxons taking place in the 5th
Century. If, therefore, there was an actual Arthur and he had a
magician-adviser called Merlin or Myrddin, it was not the bard. There
seems to be three possibilities: one is that Nennius is right and the
magician attached to Vortigern and then Arthur is Ambrosius, a name
that certainly betrays Roman antecedents. The second is that it is Geoffrey, although writing so much later, who is right, perhaps because he
had access to sources not available to the earlier historian. The third and
most likely one is that over the course of the centuries, the names of a 5th
Century warrior-hero and a 6th Century bard had come to be associated
together, because each in his way personified past glories, a time when
magicians ruled the earth.

Without doubt two late poets reflect very closely the ethos of Druidism. One is Taliesin; the other Myrddin. We know that bards and
Druids were once, if not actually united, at least very close. As I shall
argue in my next chapter, there is good reason for thinking that as far as

Wales was concerned "bard" had become virtually synonymous with "Druid".

Already in Nennius' time an infant-prodigy, like Taliesin, by Geoffrey's time Merlin has acquired another magical credential: miraculous birth. This is another similarity with Taliesin, though compared with his strictly Druidic sequence from Gwyon to the grain of corn which makes Kerridwen pregnant, Merlin's is comparatively straightforward: he comes from the womb of a princess seduced by an incubus. In all subsequent accounts this beginning is attributed to him.

We can say then that whoever Arthur's court-magician was, Merlin, as we have come to know him, is a character burdened by an encrustation of legend.

Vortigern has an eldest son whose name is given to us as Guortemir or Vortemir. In fact, this is not a name but a title. The prefix *Vor-* means "great" (Vor-tigern is actually "Great Lord") and "emir" is probably a form of "emhyr" meaning emperor, but it used in this connexion, and later in connexion with Arthur, as meaning "commander-in-chief". "Guortemir" is probably not the original "Arthur", but he could be one of the personae in a composite character.

Unlike his father, the son has challenged the invaders on the field of battle and succeeds in pushing them back to the coast. Finally, himself mortally wounded, he tells his followers that provided his body is buried at a port there will be no further incursions. For reasons which are unclear this is not done and he is interred inland, at Lincoln. As a consequence, the Saxons immediately recommence their advance.

Once more threatened, Vortigern, who has apparently left his Welsh hideout, typically prefers the way of negotiation and appeasement. Hengist appears ready to accept peace and invites his former enemies to a banquet where, however, he has all but Vortigern slaughtered. As the price of his life, the Celtic king gives three provinces to the invaders and retires, once and for all, to his mountain fastness, where finally he perishes in a fire. The event has, incidentally, strong correspondences with the burning sacrifices practised by the Druids and one is left considering whether one does not have here a reversion to the archaic royal sacrifices.

There are already signs of a tendency westwards among the still resisting Celtic forces. This may to some extent have been because the Welsh mountains offered them an ideal place from which to pursue what was really a species of guerrilla warfare, but it may also have been because it was here that there was to be found the principal centres of the old religion. Not only was Anglesey in this direction, but so was Stonehenge, while Geoffrey of Monmouth mentions a college of astronomers at Caerleon-on-Usk.

It was in this general region that the Saxons suffered defeat at the Battle of Mount Badon. The event itself is undoubtedly historical and is referred to by both the 6th Century Gildas and by Nennius, though its site remains uncertain. Suggestions include Bath, Badbury near Swindon, Badbury Hill near Faringdon and Badbury Rings near Blandford. It is here that Arthur flickers briefly into the light of history. He is mentioned as a great warrior in the *Triads of Britain* and in the 7th Century Welsh poem *Gododdin*.

The most informative, however, is Nennius who speaks of him as *dux bellorum* at the Battle of Mount Badon. The word *dux*, from which our own *duke* comes, actually means "leader", hence he was a war-leader or army commander. Although he is spoken of as a member of a league of British kings, he is not himelf titled "king" by Nennius, and, it was of course, normal Celtic practice to appoint as war-leader one not himself a king, to guard against jealousies.

This then is the bare historical foundation. It would be nice if archaeology could help us to clothe it. Sadly it is of as little assistance in pronouncing on Arthur as it is in locating Mount Badon. The only relic we have is the very dubious discovery of the remains of a man and a woman buried in the precincts of Glastonbury Abbey made by the monks in the 12th Century, a time when the Arthurian craze was at its height. With so many places, from Cornwall to Scotland, competing for the honour of burial place, the only extra qualification Glastonbury possesses is that it was probably the Avalon of the stories.

Mercifully, we are spared from the necessity of entering the debate on the historicity of Arthur or any of the other characters in the cycle. Our concern is with what is virtually the precise opposite: the way in which fact was cast aside or ignored by the various authors. This can only have been because they had previously established in their minds exactly what they wanted to make of Arthur and his legends.

What we seem to have in him is Cu Chulainn risen again to the point where one sometimes catches oneself wondering if they are not one and the same, whether perhaps names have been changed or Arthur is providing the British with the national hero they had hitherto envied the Irish for possessing. The Mórrígan, the Great Queen, who figures so frequently in Irish texts can only be the Morgan le Fay, herself a powerful queen, besides being sister to the king, in the Arthurian. This similarity extends down to their spouses. In *The Cattle Raid* we are first told that Cu Chulainn's wife is Emer, but at the end of the story he receives in marriage, Finnabair. The resemblance becomes clear when one realizes that the accepted pronunciation of "Finnabair" is actually "Finn-av-eer", that "g-" and "gw-" sounds of the Brythonic Celtic spoken in Britain were invariably rendered as an "f"- sound in the Goidelic Celtic of Ireland and Scotland, and that "Guin-" and "Finn-" both mean

White. What is more the tablet found over the alleged graves of Arthur and Guinevere at Glastonbury describe her as his second wife, as Finnabair was second wife to Cu Chulainn, though in the first case there is no reference to a first wife and in the second Emer is never clearly disposed of.

The Irish Finnabair, however, is the daughter of a goddess, Medb, divine wife of King Aillil against whom Cu Chulainn strives throughout the epic-cycle. This appears to bring Arthur within the ambit of the Celtic gods. It is possible, of course, for two women to have the same name and indeed for a mortal one to receive the name of a goddess: Diana is a ready and obvious example. But when it comes to the Welsh stories in which Arthur figures we find that identifiable Celtic gods, in the main those of the *Tuatha de Danann* form at least a sizable minority of his associates. The earliest narrative in which he occurs is *How Culhwch Won Olwen*, whose written form dates from AD 1000 at the earliest to about the mid-13th Century af the latest. Here we find—to mention only those with whom we have become familiar in these pages: Manawydan (Manannan), three sons of Dana—Hyveidd, Amathaon and Govannon —Mabon ap Modron, Llud (Nudd/Nuada/Nodens) of the Silver Hand, in addition to various sons of gods like Glinyeu son of Taran, Gwynn and Edern sons of Nudd and Rhun son of Beli, who may mean little since every self-respecting Celt claimed descent from a god. So son, like "Mac-", merely meant "descendant of". There is besides, the supernatural boar Twre Trwyth and it is a slight shock to find also none other than Conchobhar mac Nessa, king of Ulster, lurking unmistakably under the name of Cynchwr ap Nes. In Medieval Wales we are at once in the midst of a pagan Celtic ethos perhaps dating back to the 1st Century AD. This is indeed like finding Moses had got into the Wars of the Roses, to misquote the Clerihew.

The pagan Celtic ambiance is also unmistakable. Arthur is described as the foster-brother of his seneschal, Kai, and we know fosterage to have been a Celtic practice referred to by Caesar and mentioned in the myths. Enemies meet in single combat as they do in the Irish epics. The slain loser is invariably beheaded. The recurrent celebratory banquets are paralleled in the Irish stories, as they were in actual Celtic life. The Round Table emphasizes that relationship of *primus inter pares* between king and knights which we know to have been the one occupied by the chieftain. The Seat Perilous can only be that place reserved for champions which others took only if they were prepared to challenge him to combat.

The Grail may well be descended from those magic cauldrons which restore life to the fallen or provide limitless sustenance, like the cauldron of the Dagda. One remembers, too, the custom of converting skulls into drinking vessels and the link with health and life demonstrated by their presence in curative wells.

In every respect, Arthur resembles the classical Celtic warrior-hero, inhabitant of a realm in which gods and mortals rub shoulders and where there are no fixed boundaries between the worlds of living and dead. Those mysterious castles, deep in forests and shrouded in mist, are plainly the *sidhs*; their even more mysterious occupants, the Other World creatures. Thus every visit is attended by peril, the most real of perils in that one may never again emerge into the daylight of the living.

Is there not something which smacks of transmigration in the promise that Arthur will one day return?

And in the accepted tradition of Celtic kingship he has his goddess-wife, Guinevere. This might be one interpretation of the description of her as his "second wife": it is only our own, strictly monogamous ideas, which lead us to jump to the conclusion that a second wife must mean one who had succeeded another.

But far more than Cu Chulainn, Arthur traverses all the frontiers, first of the Celtic world, then of Christendom at large: Wolfram von Eschenbach's German version of *Parzifal* appeared as early as the 12th Century.

While it may well have been that it was British refugees from the Saxon invaders, finding their way to Armorica, who carried the stories of the king to the French mainland, it cannot have been a case of exiles carrying their culture to the new land. That Brittany was already associated in their minds with the stories is indicated not only by the high incidence of place-names associated with them, but by the belief—still very much alive—that real events took place in them. Two obvious examples are the Forest of Broceliande and *Le Val Sans Retour*, both shown in guidebooks and whose present-day populations are ever ready to regale one with stories associating them with Arthur. German emigrants to the United States, say, from the town of Hameln would naturally take with them the story of the famous Pied Piper. They might even settle in a town which was called Hameln or Hamelin in America. They would scarcely be deceived into believing that it was the venue of the actual event. One has to assume, therefore, that the present people of Brittany and their forebears are perfectly sincere (even if, conceivably, mistaken) in believing that these are historical sites.

And, in point of fact, there could be a connexion between Arthur and the continent. The authors of the legends appear to regard Armorica as little more than an extension of Britain, the veritable Petit Bretagne which was its original name. Geoffrey himself speaks of Arthur leading two expeditions into Europe. In the first of these he takes Gaul, giving Normandy to Bedivere and Anjou to Kai. It is also clear that he holds in cliency Hoel, King of Armorica, who is present and supports Arthur at a conference at which plans are laid for a second invasion. The object of this is to exact retribution from the Roman procurator, Lucius, for his insolent demand for the payment of outstanding tribute. There is a brief reference to this same incident in an early Welsh triad where, once again, Arthur is mentioned as going to the continent. The failure to pay tribute, at least, may have a historical foundation even if the expedition to the continent is fantasy or legend.

If it did take place, however, it may well have had a totally different motive. In Geoffrey, other Celtic lands show the greatest eagerness to assist Arthur and one wonders if his true purpose was one of liberation. For it was not only the British who were suffering from Saxon incursion: they were also harassing Gaul, which into the bargain had experienced invasion by the Franks and the horrors of dynastic struggle which had almost totally depopulated the Armorican peninsula.

By the victory at Mount Badon the British had probably secured their defence line and given themselves a breathing space. It might well have seemed prudent to Arthur to use it to neutralize potential threats on the flank, while at the same time appearing as saviour of his fellow Celts.

As we know, Arthur was mortally wounded fighting Mordred at the Battle of Camlann, another uncertain site which may be near Cadbury. The Welsh triad just cited describes Mordred (Medrawt) as being the regent appointed by Arthur, but who usurped his crown while "he was beyond the seas".

It could well be, therefore, that the association of the legends with the French mainland has come about because Arthur—whether an actual man, another to whom his name has been attached or even a composite—actually did make forays there.

One would expect a late Celtic Heroic Age, however fleeting, to be commemorated wherever it manifested itself and this must obviously be one reason for the recurrence of Arthurian connexions. In the early decades of the 12th Century, according to Hermann of Tournai, Breton monks visiting Cornwall were disputing with the natives Arthur's exact place of origin. The Cornish still dispute the point with the Welsh; the Bretons with the French.

But such nostalgia for glories past can hardly account for the lasting influence exerted by the legends on Western ideas and behaviour. The exploits of the knights of the Round Table—whether we take them from Malory or from earlier exemplars—provide, in fact, a series of latterday models set up for schoolboys down the ages. The virtuous warrior, the knight *sans peur et sans reproche*, has been emulated alike by the Crusaders and the young airmen of the Battle of Britain.

As Markale points out, great emphasis is placed on the Christian festivals and Arthur's scrupulous observance of them. For all that we may remember that they descend from pagan ones, the prevailing impression is still that of a devout prince.

Yet the ideals of self-sacrificial gallantry which charge the stories and which provide in theory, if more rarely in practice, our own accepted paradigms are, nevertheless, those of a Celtic society as it had existed for centuries before Arthur. So, too, is the high vision of romantic love which was to inform the Amour Courtois tradition. At root, of course, it is no more than that state of affairs in which human beings are free to choose in matters of love and marriage. This freedom always existed alike for women as for men in Celtic society. In a charming passage called "Pillow Talk" in *The Cattle Raid of Cooley*, the Queen Medb tells King Ailill that her need is for a man equal to her in generosity, boldness and spirit, most of all free of all taint of jealousy, for, as she tells him with remarkable candour, "I never had one man without another waiting in his shadow". And she goes on, "I got the kind of man I wanted: Rus Ruad's son—yourself, Ailill". As that passage so well demonstrates, Celtic women had "character". One thinks of Boudicca and Cartimandua, to say nothing of Emer, or of Etain or Derdriu. No dolly-birds these, content to adorn the jump-seat of a young man's sports car—and keep their mouths well and truly shut. Nor, for that matter, is Arthur's Guinevere.

At one level, the stories have to be taken as the survival of an aspect of Druidism. The Druids were guardians of myth. The old pagan deities are present even in versions as late as Malory's. What is so startling is the ease with which they can coexist with Christianity, even as it was accepted and practised by the late Middle Ages. The answer, of course, is that Celtic Christianity was a very special brand, at least arguably closer to the original vein.

Certainly the Celtic Church was very different from others. Perhaps more fundamentalist and austere, always closer to the people and their needs, its clergy were beloved and learned men. And even here, in a religion traditionally antifeminist, there was greater equality for women than elsewhere. An extant letter of the 6th Century sent to two Breton priests, Lovocat and Catihern, warns them to cease the practice of celebrating mass with the assistance of a woman. These women-priests, called *conhospitae*, administered the wine while the male priest distributed the wafers. It was not until Christianity became a state religion under Constantine and in this form was forced upon the rest of the west by Charlemagne that the priest was transmogrified into a servant of the secular state—a situation quite unknown to the Celts, incidentally, even in pagan times. As far as the people were concerned it brought with it also that pluralism whereby ecclesiastics held temporal titles and even feudal fiefs.

It is surely noteworthy that the Celts were among the first to embrace the Reformations, and that it was in Wales, Scotland, Northern Ireland, the Isle of Man and the Channel Islands that it went furthest.

Can this, at least in part, have been due to some lingering effect upon the Celtic mind of Druidic ideas? There is little doubt that the more fundamentalist Protestant sects can legitimately be described as possession-cults, indeed they would have gloried in the description. In letters after a visit to the Isle of Man, John Wesley is full of praise for the zeal of its people; in Jersey, where Huguenot priests were being appointed to the rectorship of St Helier from the mid-15th Century and continued to hold office even through the Marian counter-Reformation, he found so many followers he soon had to appoint a French-speaking pastor for his flock. This "shamanistic" aspect must have been most noticeable in the early days when, prohibited from permanent buildings, they held their meetings in the open air, often in remote places where they would be free from harassment.

And is there not a note of fatalism which might be called Calvinistic in Druidism? It is certainly present in the Cu Chulainn stories. John Steinbeck, who died while working on a version of the *Morte d'Arthur* for modern readers, notes something akin to the Greek spirit running through the book. When Arthur suggests to Merlin that knowledge of the future must enable a man to take evasive action, the old magician points to his own case. Though he knows perfectly well how he is to meet his death, he knows also that when the time comes he will also be helpless to resist it—as proved the case.

If one regards the advent of Protestantism as one of the great watersheds in the struggle for freedom of the human spirit, one must surely acknowledge that at least some of its roots had been implanted by Druidism. If we put this in the scale pan beside the effects which mythology as expressed through the Arthurian legends have had upon our civilization, one has to acknowledge a very considerable debt to the Celtic past.

And it is, of course, an enduring one. Proof of this lies not only in their continuing popularity—hardly a year passes without their reappearance in one form or another, and by no means always as "children's stories"—it lies also in the relevance found in them by succeeding generations, whose manner of life is so different from that of the times in which they came into being. We need only remind ourselves that the *Morte d'Arthur* was one of the first books to come off Caxton's press.

When he was trying to find a name for that experience through which, he believed, every male child passed, Freud recalled Sophocles's drama *Oedipus*. We now, of course, generally recognize that the profound effect the work has upon us arises very largely from its ability to touch forces deep in our unconscious. One cannot avoid the feeling that something of the sort is at work in the Arthurian legend, indeed, with most of the great Celtic myths, for all the distortions that have come down to us.

It is very much as if the Druids had struck chords in the human mind whose resonance lingers. Nowhere is this better exemplified than in those numerous stories in which the potency of an older man is threatened when a younger one begins to pay court to his daughter or daughter-surrogate. It is well known that fathers of daughters often go through a psychological crisis at this time.

Another interesting example of Celtic insight is given by Eliade in his *Images and Symbols*. The Fisher-King has fallen sick and, in typical Celtic fashion, his illness affects the entire environment. Towers crumble, gardens wilt, animals cease to breed, the springs no longer flow, there are no fruit on the trees. Every attempt is made to find a cure. All fail, until a young knight called Parsifal (probably, the Peredur of the early Welsh tales) burst in among the courtiers. He asks one question: Where is the Grail? The question is enough. The king rises from his bed and the dying world around him reawakens.

"The world is perishing", says Eliade, "because of . . . metaphysical indifference." The mere asking of the question is enough to show that that indifference is gone.

And in a deep sense that notion is inherent in Druidic ideas. They were, as Caesar tells us, much given to metaphysical speculation. So we find Arthur's knights venturing even into the bourne of death in quests whose stated objectives are always quite different from their true ones. And it cannot be otherwise. You can ask the question, what is human destiny—where is the Grail? But it has yet to be answered. Or, at least, every human individual has the choice either of ignoring it, in which case he is as moribund as was the Fisher-King, or going out to find his own answer or, more probably, only some hint of it.

CHAPTER FOURTEEN

The Immortal Magician

A contemporary American manual on magic describes in detail how the magician carries out the conjuration of spirits. Long and exacting preparations are first necessary, the slightest imperfection or the minutest omission in their execution leading to failure. The magician must fast and meditate for the previous nine days, eating only one meal of bread and water. Every detail of the robes he must wear is surrounded by detailed instructions as to the materials from which they are to be made (it must be purest linen or silk, spun by a virgin!) The words and glyphs which appear on robe, magical wand and hat (made from virgin parchment), are to be written with a pen cut from the first feather from the right wing of swallow or goose, in ink made to a specific recipe.

Everything must be done at the right time. The wand, for instance, has to be cut from a hazel-tree and must be gathered in the day and hour of Mercury. The black trumpet which the magician ritually sounds to the four points of the compass must be fumigated in an incense appropriate to the planet governing the day. Every stage of this intricate process has to be accompanied by incantations and spells. Finally, and with no less care for detail, the magician prepares his pentacle, the magical form in which he must stand, as he performs the crowning act, that of conjuration.

Such ceremonials can be traced back in Europe as far as the 15th Century when, indeed, they enjoyed something of a scandalous vogue among the wealthy. In fact, what they demonstrate is a hodge-podge of borrowings from many sources. In the spells dog-Latin is mixed freely with dog-Hebrew and even, according to at least one writer, Basque. In the various signs and hieroglyphs as shown in the book's illustrations one can see the influences of Persian and possibly, as is claimed of them, Babylonic. Yet there is, all said and done, a strangely familiar ring about it all. One thinks of the almost obsessive Brahminic preoccupation with ritual detail so that a single stone of an altar misplaced by a hair's breadth can nullify the whole proceedings. But even more one can detect clear signs of the Druids. Pliny tells us that the British Druids invested their magic with such ceremony, "that it almost seems as though it was they who had imparted the cult to the Persians".

The nine days stipulated as the period of fasting recalls that it is the square of three, the sacred number of the Druids, as the wand of hazel-wood, one of the materials they most favoured, recalls that they, too, used such a one. Mercury is the Roman equivalent of Lugh who is himself a magician and is actually connected with the hazel in some contexts. The pentacle also has the nickname of the "Druid's foot" and occurs in Celtic myth down to the 15th Century when, in the story of Gawain and the Green Knight, it forms the pattern on the hero's shield.

As so much of Celtic belief has survived, can it be that its masters and ideologues have also survived in some form?

Kendrick asserts that the very name "Druid", like the possessors of it, perished in AD 62 on the fires they had lit for their own sacrificial victims and did not reappear until the 18th Century revival. He acknowledges, however, that the stone found in Man with the word translated as "Druid" upon it dates only from the 5th or 6th Century. He also refers to the use of the word in the Irish version of the *Historia Brittonum* where the magicians of Vortigern are so described, though he points out that this is a late rendering and the original term was "magicians".

The view of a total eclipse of Druidism looks very much less tenable now than when Kendrick was writing in the nineteen-twenties, for all that we must acknowledge the latterday Druids are much changed, emasculated we might fairly say. The course Vortigern's magicians advocated, that of sacrificing a child and burying its body in the foundations of his fortress to ensure its impregnability is undoubtedly Druidic. A body found during excavations at Aulnay-aux-Planches in France is probably that of a sacrificed infant. There is a child's grave at Wood Henge, and I am indebted to Geoffrey Ashe for pointing out another example at Silbury. The concept even managed to penetrate Christianity apparently, for when St Columba was building his first church on the Scottish Island of Iona one of his associates volunteered to be buried alive to make sure the edifice stood.

There is also the mystery of the Saxon massacre of the British chiefs by Hengist. Of this there are a number of variants. One, occurring in a poem by an unknown early Welsh poet, locates the event in a circle of stone, possibly Stonehenge, though of course there were other such circles. Here a festival is taking place which includes the free flow of wine and mead. From other sources it is possible to conclude that it took place early in May which would make it correspond with the feast of Beltain. As we know Stonehenge to be associated with solar observation and Belenos to be ruling god of the sun, celebrations there on the day of his festival are extremely probable. We have in addition the evidence of Hecateus mentioned in Chapter Eleven that there was a temple, dedicated to Apollo, in an island plainly identifiable as Britain.

It was, furthermore, a common tactic for the Saxons to swoop on their enemies during religious festivals. It is probable, too, that Vortigern, aging and traditionalist in outlook, not only sought Druidic advice, but also kept up the important festivals.

This would bring Druidism down to the 5th Century, but we know also that the early Celtic saints were exercised by the problem of ridding society of the last tenacious traces of paganism. "Christ is my Druid," proclaims St Columba, a cry hardly likely to have evoked much response if the order had been forgotten. We know, as in the case of the Channel Island saint, Sampson, that it was necessary to go to the lengths of bribing children to keep them from attending pagan festivals. A 10th Century law of King Edgar forbade "well-worshippings, necromancies and divinations; enchantments and man-worshippings, and all other vain practices which are carried out with various spells"—a list of observances possessing an unmistakably Druidic character. The prohibition on well-worshipping, at least, seems to have been peculiarly ineffective, since, under the auspices of the church it still continues in several places.

And what is to be made of the Merlin-Arthur duality? For all that he was a latecomer to the stories and whoever his prototype may have been he certainly seems to carry with him impeccable Druidic credentials. This is not a matter of chance or because magicians, however they may title themselves, are still magicians and very much alike. Merlin, throughout, occupies a position in relation to Arthur which largely parallels that of the great Druids like Cathbadh or Mac Roth in the Irish stories. He plays the traditional role of chooser of the king, making his choice manifest through a miraculous sign; he changes shape and imparts the gift of doing so to others, as in the case of Uther Pendragon's seduction of Ygraine; he prophesies; he provides magical weapons; the spirits he invokes come up from beneath the waters; he is under a *geas* which leads to his own humiliating destruction.

The list of parallels could well be amplified and their existence becomes the more astonishing when one considers that Geoffrey, in whose work Merlin first appears, was writing at least a thousand years after the fall of Anglesey had supposedly brought Druidism to its end. One cannot escape the impression that the authors or the sources from whom they had borrowed knew very well what Druidic magic was and that their readers can scarcely have been ignorant of it either. Indeed, such a conclusion seems to me the only strictly logical one, since if the people of Man were talking of herb-doctors like the 19th Century Teare Bellawhane as a "successor of the Druids", how much more must those living in the 12th Century have thought in such terms.

In so far as the word "Druid" could be said to have disappeared it was, surely, because of the fundamental changes the language was undergoing. There was the spread of Saxon influence while the tongue of the literate élite became Latin. This was followed by the arrival of the Normans and the spread of French. What had actually been lost, though only to the world of scholarship, was the Celtic language. Their separation from it is shown by the frequent mistakes made in translation, mistakes which, incidentally, have sometimes survived to our times.

One can safely assume that this was why the word "Druid" had become incomprehensible and had been replaced by another, familiar one.

But, in any case, words are lost surprisingly easily. The pages of the Oxford Dictionary are littered with those which are followed by the rubric "obs." for "obsolete". One example, though from a possible myriad, suffices. As late as the eighteen-eighties, the word "Kickshaw" meaning literally an elegant or fancy dish, but extended to figurative connotations, was in common usage, employed among others by Dickens. Who now knows it, let alone uses, it?

Nor is the statement that the word "Druid" disappeared strictly true. There is evidence that in at least three Celtic tongues it continued in use. In Manx Celtic, the word "Druaight" plainly has a connexion and "Droat", actually meaning "Druid" remained in use until the language itself disappeared. In Ireland as we have seen, it was still current in the 9th Century. In the early 18th Century, a Protestant minister in Skye wrote his *Description of the Western Islands of Scotland*. He uses the word "Druid" for the man who conducted a clan ceremony—that of giving the chieftain's son his arms; a precisely similar ritual was carried out by the Druids of pagan times. It is obvious from his use of the word that the author was following the practice of the people he is describing.

There are good reasons for believing that in Wales the word "bard" for a long time connoted "Druid" (or, of course, magician), as in Scotland for an equal period the word "Druid" may well have been applied to those who in many ways were carrying out bardic functions.

Roman influence did not extend to Scotland so that there was no reason why men should not continue to call themselves Druids there. In Wales, matters stood differently, for Druidism was under Roman proscription. By taking up their harps and calling themselves "bards" they were probably able to circumvent the letter of the occupiers' law. Such subterfuges are well known to all those who have suffered enemy occupation, as I can personally testify. Certainly, if Myrddin is the proto-Merlin, he was officially a bard, and though he prophesied he concealed his gift under an appearance of madness.

Taken all in all, one surely has to concede that one is confronted by something more than sheer chance survivals of Druidism, cases comparable, say, with that of the court mourning ordered at the death of Queen Anne which somehow managed to live on to become the wig and gown still worn by English judges and barristers. Unaided chance can hardly have been responsible in this case, for to have come down to us, the customs and practices described here had to outlive not only Christianization, but both Roman and Saxon invasions before that, a period covering in all some six centuries. And how little, by comparison, the ideas of either have taken root!

The Romans, whose declared purpose was to destroy Celtic religion through its ministers, the Druids, had so far to admit failure as to allow the gods of their subject peoples to stand side by side with their own. The early Christian missionaries make it clear that Celtic paganism was very much alive at the time of their arrival from about 600 AD. They refer, specifically, to Druids.

One can speculate as to the course of events without risking too great a divergence from the facts. Roman occupation undoubtedly drove the Druids underground. I pointed out in Chapter Twelve that they had probably already lost much of their political power and possibly a measure of their religious dominance, too. Since, however, the Romans were not replacing Celtic religion by any dynamically new system, it is unlikely that there was any large scale abandonment. On the contrary, persecution would probably have touched the Druids with a heroic glamour in most people's eyes. But they were besides and before all else magicians, and the mark of their craft is that it is concerned primarily with specific and individual problems such as were beyond the skill and beneath the dignity of priests ministering to a religion in the true sense. (Though we know, of course, that the later Christian fathers took over functions like teaching and care of the sick.) One would expect, therefore, that those particular problems would seek them out. But, there was, anyway, for the fugitive Druids the question of gaining a livelihood. Fees for their services, in money or kind, would be one means of survival.

The departure of the Romans even after three hundred years of their presence, would have made possible a return to that "true Celticism" for which, no doubt, many had romantically yearned. In this situation, Druidism might well have enjoyed something of a temporary resurgence. If this did not include the repossession of political power in the sense they had once enjoyed it, their purely practical knowledge as physicians, astronomers, calendarists, possibly as expert metal-workers, even as natural philosophers would have come into their own once more. No doubt, too, their magical advice was taken by rulers on more than the single occasion when Vortigern is thought to have followed it.

The next threat was, of course, the coming of Christianity, but we must be clear about its effects on Celtic paganism. The missionaries were few in number and their successes can only have been limited. Even in the areas where these were greatest, the changes brought about would have been less sweeping than they are usually imagined to have been.

Whenever one examines at close quarters the lives of ordinary men and women through the great epochs of history—the Reformation, the Renaissance, the French Revolution—one is always struck by two things. One is their apparent indifference to what is going on around them or, when directly affected, their capacity for adapting. The other, even more striking one, is the human ability to modify the most radical new ideas, so that even the profoundest of changes quickly acquires the patina of things familiar. To say that the traces of old habits and ways of thinking survive from one regime to its successor is totally to understate the process: more often it is the new ideas themselves which seem to become mere traces. Perhaps the innate conservatism of the human baulks at too great an upheaval threatening to deprive it of the consolation of the known and familiar.

So when Christianity replaced the Old Religion, the gods simply took on fresh names, those of saints, and in this guise were worshipped at festivals which had gone on for centuries perhaps even before Celtic times. Such practices as human sacrifice had been banned by the Romans; it had no doubt gone on in secret, but was probably declining anyway. And when it came to the things that really mattered like curing an outbreak of boils or a lame cow or discovering what the future might hold, the ordinary man and his wife knew exactly where to apply.

It may be going too far to suggest that a writer as late as Malory knew of and used as his prototype for Merlin surviving magical practitioners, though, since they were still to be found centuries later, they must have existed and in greater profusion in his day. It is certainly in Malory that Merlin achieves his fullest development, not only as a rounded character, but as a magician in an overtly Druidic sense.

Malory is himself a mystery, however. There are no fewer than four candidates for the authorship of *The Morte d'Arthur:* A Welshman; a Huntingdonshire country gentleman; a wilder Thomas Malory known to have lived at Newbold Revel in Warwickshire, and a man of the same name from Ripon, Yorkshire. What we know, from his own testimony, is that at the time of writing he was in prison for an unspecified act of "turbulency against the king". This sounds as if he might have played a minor role in some revolt (if it had been a major role his punishment would have been more serious than imprisonment), but, on the other hand, the Newbold Revel Thomas Malory is known to have practised burglary, abduction and rape and been brought to trial for these acts which, naturally, makes him the favoured candidate of many scholars. The difficulty here is a psychological one: how does one reconcile the vicious criminal with the *Morte d'Arthur* itself, which certainly contains more than its measure of violence, but mixes it with chivalric gallantry, compassion and piety?

It is tempting to identify him with the Welshman, and the equation has certainly been made. Unfortunately, however, he specifically describes himself as one "of us Englysshemen", an obstacle which no amount of ingenious argument has wholly been able to overcome.

In one of the most recent books on the subject, *The Ill-Framed Knight* the Professor of English at Berkeley University, William Matthews, presses the claim of the Yorkshire Sir Thomas with great skill and literary elegance. The proposition is at least a beguiling one, since the *Morte d'Arthur* appeared in a period when the Wars of the Roses were first fomenting and when England was ruled by a Lancastrian monarch.

From what he tells us about himself Malory would have been in his impressionable teens when some very dramatic events were taking place in Wales. Owein Glendwr, who claimed descent from Llewellyn, last Prince of Wales, had launched a highly successful revolt against the English king, Henry IV.

One would expect sympathy for this to run most strongly in Wales, but in England, too, partisanship was considerable and national loyalty divided. Henry IV had gained the throne by usurpation from Richard II, son of the Black Prince. The basis of his claim was so insubstantial that once the throne was secured he made no real effort to justify it. Feeble, inept and treacherous as Richard had often shown himself to be, he nevertheless commanded an appreciable and loyal following. This was not easily to be silenced: a session of the House of Lords shortly after Henry's accession broke up in disorder as peers partial to one contender or the other slung gauntlets across the chamber, and was saved from degenerating into an open brawl only by the king's personal intercession.

Glendwr was among Richard's most devoted supporters. He had actually been taken prisoner with him by Henry's forces and released only on the king's surety. He had retired to his Welsh estates, to be mulcted of property in England by members of Henry's party, an act which provided his immediate incitement to revolt.

It was rapidly to acquire a nationalist complexion, but that it had been an attempt to depose Henry is shown by the challenge thrown out by the insurgents, in accordance with the laws of chivalry, before one of the key battles. This declared Henry to be not only a usurper, but a "false and perjured knight"—echoes of the Round Table. At the end of its list of charges it closed: "For these reasons we do mortally defy thee and thy accomplices and adherents, as traitors, and subverters of the commonwealth and kingdom, and invaders, oppressors and usurpers of the rights of the true and direct heir of England and France; and we intend to prove it this day by force of arms with the aid of Almighty God". The battle ended, of course, in Glendwr's defeat, though not his extinction, for he was to continue his fight, sporadically, into the reign of Henry V. He is believed to have died about the time of the Battle of Agincourt, that is to say in 1415, at the home of his daughter in Herefordshire.

We have no direct evidence that Malory belonged to Henry's opponents save only that if he did not it is very strange that he should have chosen to write a book about a great Celtic heroic age and a running struggle against an ambitious conqueror. Furthermore, the circumstances in which Arthur lost his throne and ultimately his life very closely parallel those in which Richard lost his. Arthur was abroad fighting when Mordred seized the kingship; Richard was in Ireland attempting to quell a revolt when Henry seized his.

But the name of Owein Glendwr is important for another and most intriguing reason. Born at Merioneth in 1349, he was indeed the great grandson of Llewellyn, but had been educated in London at one of the Inns of Court. He had been called to the English Bar, but quickly came to the notice of the king and was made an esquire in his court. A brilliant figure in courtly life, he had married Margaret, the daughter of Sir David Hanmer, a King's Bench judge and at the age of thirty-eight was knighted.

But he was, as we also know, closely associated with magical practice. One may look with suspicion on theories like those of the late Margaret Murray which have a whole succession of English kings involved in witch-craft, fertility cults and even of complicity in their own ritual sacrifice (William Rufus, is of course, supposed to be the classical instance). This does not alter the fact that in this particular case, Owein was probably practising his craft as early as his London days and that his patrons included Richard II.

Certainly, in the time of his rebellion the English inability to bring about his final defeat was freely ascribed by both friend and foe to his occult skill. He was known to spend large sums on "bards" and, through them, claimed to be the realization of the prophecies of Merlin who had forecast that he was to destroy Henry "the moldwarp accursed of God's own wrath".

In one battle, the English troops claimed that they had been unsuccessful because their enemy had summoned up a heavy rainstorm, making the scaling of the mountains to reach his hideouts impossible. On several occasions they were stopped in their advance by spell-casters bawling their imprecations down at them, practices similar to those mentioned by both Strabo and Tacitus in connexion with the Druids.

What we see in Owein, therefore, is the continuation of a number of Druidic traditions. His claim to descent from Llewellyn is traced in the maternal line, for example, but more significant is the association of magician and warrior-chief, though now in merged form, which he obviously exemplifies. As the early Irish heroes have their Druids, Arthur his Merlin, so he partly fulfils the magical role himself. Plainly, as leader of the Welsh national revival, the main reason for his involvement in these practices was because it was what would have been expected of him. Nor could he have practised any other form of magic than that of his Celtic forebears, the Druids. Furthermore, if my equation of the later Welsh bards with some sort of survival of Druidism is correct, then we can see he was surrounding himself with those who were probably at least in part magicians.

Owein Glendwr has a second claim upon us: he is regarded as spiritual ancestor by many of the witchcraft cults now practising in Britain. To take the claims of these groups at face value would, of course, put far too great a strain on credulity. As Frank Smyth, author of a book on contemporary witchcraft points out, their milieu is suburbia, their membership drawn largely from the lower middle class whose roots are urban. Even in the case of the Manx witch covens, those running or patronising them are mostly newcomers to the island. They are besides a recent phenomenon. Frank Smyth says it is difficult to trace their beginnings back earlier than 1949.

This is a slight exaggeration. Modern magic and witchcraft in Britain have two immediate progenitors: Aleister Crowley, who rejoiced in the title of "The Beast 666" from the Apocalypse and Gerald Gardner, so-called "King of the British Witches". Crowley, born in 1875 and who died in 1947, was strictly speaking more black magician than witch, though his influence was considerable. His Order of the Golden Dawn, mentioned in Chapter One, evolved with a type of latterday Satanist possession-cult, practising its rites at a cult centre in Sicily though also associated with Stonehenge. Its activities were of a sufficiently erotic nature to attract that press publicity their founder's vanity craved, but in substance seemed to have comprised only a mishmash of quirky notions gathered from a plethora of unrelated sources.

Gardner, who died in 1964 at the age of 80, was a later arrival on the scene and had himself been influenced by Crowley's ideas. He was the author of three books on witchcraft which purported to give details of beliefs, practices and rites derived from Medieval sources, the period when witchcraft was at its height. In fact, the book is little more than a regurgitation of other, readily available contemporary works.

At his death his vacant throne fell to Alex Sanders, who claims descent in the maternal line from none other than Owein Glendwr himself.

Gardner states in one of his books that he was converted to witchcraft by an old lady who lived near his own home at Christchurch in the New Forest, a venue traditionally redolent with magic. She persuaded him that it was a pre-Christian survival, truly the Old Religion. Alex Sanders says he was initiated into it by his grandmother, while a child in Wales. Although Gardner was quite capable of fabrication, there is little reason to doubt this particular statement and certainly none at all for doubting Alex Sanders.

And they give the whole matter an entirely changed aspect, since instead of being nothing but a mumbo-jumbo mugged up from cranky literature, it is now given roots of some sort in folklore. We need not be greatly surprised if pre-Christian religions ideas survived among isolated rural communities: it is no stranger than the survival of pagan myth; of pagan festivals like the Helston Furry Dance or of such other pagan practices as well-visiting, prophecy and even herb-medicine. Indeed, Professor Ross has discovered an entire community in Northumberland which venerates the "old gods" while still professing and practising Christianity. Its members claim that they are of Celtic stock, a remnant who refused to flee during the various migrations.

Witches have existed almost as far back as our knowledge of humanity extends. They were to be found among the Hittites and the Akkadians. Solomon, as we know, had recourse to one. But what witchcraft almost certainly represents is a shamanistic religion in a state of degeneration. It is then that, having lost intellectual credibility and hence its hold on the mass of its followers, it falls back on its old skill – that of mastering the elements of nature by means of rituals.

Properly speaking, therefore, there are not one but many witchcrafts. The witches of the Hittites, the Hebrews, Greeks or Romans each represented the survival of an earlier religion, and like the modern witches, their practitioners would have been perfectly accurate to call theirs the "Old Religion". In so far as it is possible to find similarities between these various strange relics these were no doubt brought about by similarities in the underlying religions themselves.

In view of its roots one would expect the witchcraft of the Celtic world or of those lands formerly inhabited by Celts to display markedly the elements of Druidism, and one is hardly disappointed. Modern witchcraft contains, beside a mother-goddess—who when actually named is called "Diana"—a horned god. Outsiders might equate him with Satan; the witches knew better.

Witchcraft has, of course, its strongly magical, ritualistic complexion. It frequently practises its rites in the open—where the spirits of nature are most accessible—and at night. The English word "witch" is itself at least partially cognate with "Druid", coming from the Middle English "wicca" or "wise". The various knives, daggers and swords with which witches surround themselves during their ceremonials can only bring to mind those of the Druids, used no doubt for sacrificial purposes and for divination. Even the traditional cauldron, still to be found in many groups, has it origins in the magical cauldrons of abundance and resurrection which figure so prominently in the myths and which may be the prototype of the Grail.

The persistence of such traces through the centuries is wholly consistent with the nature of Druidism itself and with the experiences the Celtic peoples underwent. We know, for instance, how Judaism provided a centre of coalescene for the Jewish peoples through all centuries of exile and persecution, while at the same time the former religious divisions disappeared (at least until our own times). The Celts, though not as a whole exiled, witnessed a species of national extinction and experienced subjugation to foreign invaders. They were not permitted to retain even their own form of Christianity, but had to submit to an alien and uncongenial one. It is only to be expected, in such circumstances, that they should turn back to the only thing with which they could identify as one—Druidism. The appearance so easily gained when contemplating them in retrospect, that the Druids were in the process of imposing a single pantheon overriding the myriad of purely local deities may be due less to any deliberate actions on their part, than to the consolidation of Celtic national ideology under the stresses of conquest and occupation. In other words, as with the Jews, differences, which, in the Celtic case were tribal, sank of their own accord before the greater external threat.

But Druidism was not a religion in any clearly understood sense: it was a magical cult. Thus to establish his credentials as national leader a man had also to prove his magical skill. He must, like Glendwr, be a magician himself, or else he must operate in close collaboration with one, like Arthur. This need to emulate is itself a tribute to the prestige of the Druids.

As a matter of fact, magic provides its own survival-kit. In Rome, although the punishment for practising it was as harsh as in Medieval Europe, magicians and witches were still to be found and enjoyed enough patronage to gain a living. There has never been an age, least of all our own, when the magician in whatever guise did not do a roaring trade. And the Druids were unusually powerful magicians, possessed of real and formidable knowledge, as we have seen.

Once persecution of witches began, those of Celtic lineage, who represented an abnormally high proportion of the total, could claim that this was merely the extension to them of the repression their people had so long suffered; that they were victims not so much on account of their arcane practices as their nationality. The accusation is not without substance; the non-Celtic peoples had the strongest dislike of witchcraft. In a number of cases, the reaction to it among Celtic nations themselves was comparatively muted. Where, as happened in Brittany, harsher measures were taken they were often imposed by outsiders. By contrast, in Guernsey and particularly in Jersey, only a few miles from the Breton coast, but always autonomous, things were quite different. Although innumerable witches were brought to trial in the 17th Century, torture was never used to extract confessions (though they confessed just the same!). Few were sentenced to death, some were merely fined. One was actually put on probation, and this in a largely Calvinist society.

The part played by Druidic influences in maintaining Celtic national identity, was combined with another, equally important factor. As I M Lewis has conclusively demonstrated with scores of examples, ecstasy and possession cults invariably spring into existence among deprived minorities. In Protestant societies this will often take the form of "revivalist" sects springing up among the poorest sections of the community. In the monolithic church of the Middle Ages this would have been inconceivable heresy. Instead the discontented reverted to something earlier or, at any rate, what they could recapture of it. The 19th Century French historian, Jules Michelet, was among the first to draw attention to the phenomenon. He describes how the French peasantry turned away from Christianity with the coming of feudalism and the accompanying suppression of the popular Celtic church in favour of one which united in tyranny clergy and aristocracy. It was in their distress that the peasantry, in isolated places and late at night, began reviving the Old Religion whose deities were the real masters of the earth and its fruits. And they, too, had a horned god.

The 13th and 14th Centuries which saw the great resurgence of witchcraft were also periods of dire hardship among the peasants and often of open revolt. There can scarcely have been a time when some group or other was not undergoing deprivation and when, therefore, it would not turn to the one force which offered hope, whose reputation had been passed down from father to son or, more probably, from mother to daughter, so that its framework always remained. There are certainly indications that witchcraft was being extensively practised during the time of the Industrial Revolution and the eras that led up to it. There was certainly a revival of interest in Druidism.

The circle has gone its full revolution: as we began with the Druids of the Celtic revival so we find ourselves back in their midst. Have we discovered anything which might lead us to suppose they were some sort of heirs to an Ancient Wisdom? Pursuing his search for it, by way of the sacred number seven, Geoffrey Ashe found it concentrated in a region beyond the Altaic mountains of Mongolia and Southern Siberia. This is the region of "The Great Bear"—the Seven Stars—to which all the signs ultimately point. "If the Ancient Wisdom did makes its way into the various cultures," he says, "this Altaic zone is the most promising place to look for its cradle-land."

Here among the Buryat peoples shamanism is still to be found, its practices surrounded by mystery and high magic. It is here, for example, that, so its people claim, thought can be turned into visible forms. (Geoffrey Ashe draws attention to a very early and well documented "Flying Saucer" appearance in this region in 1927. The natives, quite unsurprised by it, immediately described it as a thought-form.)

One must, naturally, remember that one is considering this region as it was perhaps four thousand years ago and even the Ancient Wisdom can hardly have stood quite still in all this time. Geographically, however, it was ideally placed to reach out in all directions: eastwards to Tibet and China; northwards to the Siberian steppe and the Arctic; westward to the zones forming the homelands of the Indo-European peoples.

There is every likelihood that it was the insights of Altaic proto-shamans which first revealed astronomy and mathematics to the world. Though, almost certainly, they took the forms of astrology and numerology, they still represented the first giant stride towards the concept of an ordered universe, the Cosmos of the Greeks and their successors.

But the risk of over-estimating the extent of Druidic knowledge is as great as that of underestimating it. One has always to reconcile it with such barbarities as the taking of auspices from the death throes of a stabbed man, with the selection of the king through "the bull dream", with the decapitation of enemies and the retention of their heads, with the whole emotive and elaborate ritual of the great festivals leading up to the moment of immolation of the human victim.

It would be absurd to deny that the Druids possessed real and valuable practical knowledge and complemented it, no doubt, with intelligence and native shrewdness, but it was also adulterated with much that was no more than vapid ritual and gibberish, accepted quite uncritically. The fact that they could be credited with actual knowledge and skill in some fields would no doubt have given them credibility in others. Their ability to predict astronomical events, for instance, their skill as hypnotists, as mathematicians, as herb-doctors, perhaps as water-diviners, would have tended to predispose not only those of their own times, but also those who came later, to accept their claims to prophecy or to the casting of effective spells.

This is hardly what one expects of heirs to the Ancient Wisdom, however. But then, what of the Ancient Wisdom? Perhaps, even when looking at things from an evolutionist point of view there is something of which account needs to be taken. The physical law that for every action there is a reaction, equal but opposite, must apply here too. By adopting the upright posture the primates freed their forepaws to be developed into tool- and weapon-holders. We can justly say, therefore, that this represented "an improved adaptation" in the classical Darwinian pattern. On the other hand it brought with it adversities previously unknown. In pregnancy, women had now to bear the weight of the developing embryo dangling vertically in their wombs, where, hitherto, it had lain comfortably slung beneath them. There came also a whole train of diseases of which haemorrhoids provide an apt if nasty illustration.

But in mental and cultural evolution there must have been similar losses. It is probably true that the invention of writing led to the deterioration of the memory, as the invention of printing led to fewer people learning the art of calligraphy and so to the decline of handwriting.

The gift of telepathic communication might afford an example of loss at an earlier stage. There is an abundance of examples of "primitive" peoples, such as the Australian aborigines, who retain the gift.

Many cultures make a clear distinction between ordinary dreams and visions, indicating that they place each in a separate category. This can hardly have been mere caprice, so that the distinction, surely, is this: that the vision provided some kind of revelation. Through its medium some great inductive leap was made. Almost certainly many of the numerous cases in which deities are said to be responsible for bringing this or that gift to humanity can, in the final analysis, be traced to a vision in which the deity made his appearance. In the past, the vision was trusted so implicitly that none hesitated to act upon it. Indeed, as Hadfield says, it was often regarded as more "real" than waking life. This made the visionary himself a respected member of the community, even one set above his fellows.

There is a third instance. Earlier I discussed the shamanistic practice of "spirit-flight" or ecstasy. It was probably employed by the Druids. Of course, one can easily dismiss all such phenomena as mere superstitious delusion, but this is to ignore something very similar to "spirit-flight" known to paranormal research workers. It is the so-called "astral projection" or "out-of-the-body" experience.

In two, now very well-known books, Sylvan Muldoon and Hereward Carrington have described the case-histories of scores of instances of "out-of-the-body" experiences drawn from all over the world and from something approaching a century in time. More are to be found in other

works. Typically, the subject finds himself (as he believes) separated
from his bodily self, able, indeed, to observe it as discrete entity still lying
in bed, for example. In some cases, the physical bodies appear to be dead
and have even been declared so by physicians. The subject has watched
them as they struggled with resuscitation techniques and, after returning
to his body, has even been able to describe in detail their actions and
their conversations during the period he appeared to be dead.

In its liberated state, the spirit is often able to travel great distances
and numerous instances of such journeys are recorded. In one, the subject (the Professor of English at an American university) visited the
home of friends in Los Angeles while "physically" in hospital in New
York.

These cases all show a remarkable similarity to the shaman's "spirit
flight" in which his body remains behind "a mere husk". Stranger still,
in two classical instances, those of the Dionysian and Apollonian cults,
both of which involved ecstasy, the god is said to enter the subject by
way of the head or the nape of the neck, a detail which also finds support
among the Haitian and other Voodoo-cults. Exactly this detail is given
by many of those who have had "out-of-the-body" experiences; the
"spirit" is said to have left and re-entered the body through the sagittal
suture in the crown of the head.

Taking the various instances given over these last few pages together,
all activities associated with religious practice of "primitive" peoples, it
is plain that if the existence of the phenomena described can be accepted
as established they must have possessed very great mastery of certain
types of mental process which we should call "paranormal".

To us, if we tried to explain them it would be as manifestations of the
unconscious mind. Yet, for all that it is our own discovery, we are
strangely suspicious of the unconscious. Perhaps Freud has succeeded in
making it appear as some sort of internal monster, controlled only at
great cost and no little risk.

But had the same kind of extreme caution and suspicion been shared
by other generations, much would have been lost to us.

Let us take hypnotism, a technique practised by the shamans and, no
doubt, by the Druids, and one which, in its manifestations, has a
remarkably "magical" appearance. It was discarded, we know, for centuries as pure hocus-pocus connected with such heresies as witchcraft,
and it was more or less by chance that it was revived in Paris as Franz
Mesmer's "animal magnetism". Mesmer was a charlatan within the
most precise definition of the term, reason enough to dismiss him and all
his works without for a moment degrading science by a serious examination of it.

Fortunately, there were sufficient open-minded men at the Salpetriere
to avoid just this trap. They proved it to be reproducible and so finally

convinced even the most sceptical, though not without experiencing difficulty and mockery. Things could very easily have been otherwise: a touch more scepticism and the whole thing would have been dismissed or consigned to the class of not-quite-respectable paranormal phenomena. For the fact is that hypnotism only works in the degree in which the person undergoing it believes it to do so. If he lies on the hypnotist's couch convinced nothing is going to happen, it will not happen.

One cannot avoid the feeling that had Mesmer appeared on the scene a little later than he did, there might well have been no Charcot or Braid ready to concede that perhaps, perhaps there was something here which deserved to be seriously considered. At the very best, scientists would still be arguing as to whether the phenomena had been established.

Taking all things into consideration, one might conclude that what had been lost was less an Ancient Wisdom, than what we might call "an Ancient Skill", an ability to harness the forces of the mind. Of this we have some inkling in the great Yogi and Fakirs of Hinduism whose amazing abilities are only now and very tentatively at that, being taken seriously.

Can we attribute such skills to the Druids? The parallels with the Hindu Brahmins are so astonishing and so numerous that it seems not unlikely that at least in rudimentary form they did. Like so much else the phenomena connected with trance states have hardly begun to be investigated. There are, for example, the well-attested instances where, in this condition, body weight has been significantly altered. Under hypnosis, the subject having been told his strength has increased, will lift with ease a weight he could not so much as move in a normal state. Since we have strong evidence for supposing the Druids to have interested themselves in trance-states, it is scarcely conceivable they did not experiment along these lines. There is no doubt either that the Greek preoccupation with philosophy largely took the form of a desire to discover ways in which mind could conquer matter and such demonstrations of an apparent capability in this direction would help to account for the impression the Druids, with the Brahmins and Magi and, possibly, the Babylonic priests, produced on observers like Aristotle, Aristeas or Pythagoras.

It would also account for the later denunication of Druidism and the "magical" skills of its practitioners by the Church, which would have taken them to be derived from "the Powers of Darkness".

Select Bibliography

Anwyl, E, *Celtic Religion in pre-Christian Times*, London, 1906.

Ashe, Geoffrey, *The Ancient Wisdom*, London, 1977.

Bromwick, R, *Trioedd Ynys Prydein: The Welsh Triads*, Cardiff, 1961.

Cagnat, R, *Sacred Spring of Alesia*, quoted as note in Ant. Journal, II, 147, London, 1922.

Campbell, J G, *Superstitions of the Highlands and Islands of Scotland*, Glasgow, 1900.

Campbell, J G, *Witchcraft and Second Sight in the Highlands and Islands of Scotland*, Glasgow, 1902.

Carney, J (ed.), *Early Irish Poetry*, Cork, 1965.

Chadwick, Nora, *The Celts*, Harmondsworth, 1970.

Danielou, Alain, *Hindu Polytheism*, London, 1964.

Davidson, H R E, *Pagan Scandinavia*, London, 1967.

Dillon, M, and Chadwick, N, *The Celtic Realms*, London, 1967, 1972.

Dillon, M, *Early Irish Literature*, Chicago, 1948.

Dillon, M, *Irish Sagas*, Cork, 1970.

Dillon, M, *Serglige con Culainn*, Dublin, 1953.

Dillon, M, *Tain Bo Fraich* (The Driving-Off of Fraich's Cattle), Dublin, 1933.

Dunn, J, *Tain Bo Cualnge* (The Cattle Raid of Cooley), Dublin, 1914.

Dumezil, G, *Les Dieux des Indo-Europeens*, Paris, 1952.

Dumezil, G, *Mithra-Varuna*, Paris, 1940.

Duval, P-M, *Les Dieux de la Gaule*, Paris, 1957.

Duval, P-M, *Teutates, Esus, Taranis*, Etudes Celtiques 8; 1958–9, 41–58.

Eliade, M, *Images et Symboles*, Paris, 1961.

Eliade, M, *Le Chamanisme et les Techniques Archaiques de l'Extase*, Paris, 1964.

Evans-Pritchard, E E, *Theories of Primitive Religion*, Oxford, 1965.

Evans-Wentz, W Y, *The Tibetan Book of the Great Liberation*, Oxford, 1954.

Filip, J, *Celtic Civilisation and its Heritage* (trs), 1962.

Graves, Robert, *The White Goddess*, London, 1975.

Gwynn E, *The Metrical Dindshenchas*, RIA Todd Lecture Series, IX, pt. 2, 1906; X, 1913; XI, pt IV, 1924; VII, 1900, Dublin.

Hadingham, Evan, *Circles and Standing Stones*, London, 1975.

Hamel, A G van, *Aspects of Celtic Mythology*, Rhys Lecture, Proceedings of the British Academy, XX; 207–42, 1934.

Harrison, Michael, *The Roots of Witchcraft*, London, 1972.

Hawkins, G S, *Stonehenge Decoded*, London, 1966.

Jackson, K H, *The Oldest Irish Tradition*, Cambridge, 1964.

James, E D (ed.), *The Cult of the Mother-Goddess*, London, 1959.

Kendrick, T D, *The Druids: A Study of Celtic Prehistory*, London, 1966; first ed. 1927.

Killip, Margaret, *Folklore of the Isle of Man*, London, 1975.

Kinsella, Thomas, *The Tain*, London, 1969.

Lambrechts, Pierre, *Contributions à l'Etudes des Divinites Celtiques*, Bruges, 1942.

Lambrechts, Pierre, *L'Exaltation de la Tête dans Pensée et dans l'Art des Celtes*, Bruges, 1954.

Lambrechts, Pierre, *Note sur le Passage de Gregoire de Tours relatif à la Religion Gauloise*, Latomus, 1954.

Lambrechts, Pierre, *Note sur une statuette en bronze de Mercure*, L'Antiquite Classique X, 1941. Brussels, 1946.

L'Amy, John, *Jersey Folklore*, Jersey, 1927.

Lempriere, Raoul, *Customs, Ceremonies and Traditions of the Channel Islands*, London, 1976.

Lewis, I M, *Ecstatic Religion*, Harmondsworth, 1975.

Macculloch, J A, *The Religion of the Ancient Celts*, Edinburgh, 1911.

MacNeill, Maire, *The Festival of Lughnasa*, Oxford, 1962.

Markale, Jean, *Les Celtes*, Paris, 1969.

Markale, Jean, *Le Roi Arthur*, Paris, 1976.

Markale, Jean, *Women of the Celts*, Gordon & Cremonesi, London, 1975.

Marwick, Ernest W, *The Folklore of the Orkney and Shetland Islands*, London, 1975.

Matthews, William, *The Ill-Framed Knight*, Berkeley and Los Angeles, 1966.

Maudite, J A, *L'Epopée des Celtes*, Paris, 1973.

Neumann, Erich, *The Great Mother*, London, 1955.

O'Rahilly, T F, *Early Irish History and Mythology*, Dublin, 1946.

Paine, Lauran, *Witchcraft and the Mysteries*, New York and London, 1975.

Piggott, Stuart, *The Druids*, London, 1965.

Piggott, Stuart, *The Sources of Geoffrey of Monmouth*, Antiquity, XV; 269–86; 305–19, 1941.

Powell, T G E, *The Celts*, London, 1958.

Rasmussen, K, *The Intellectual Culture of the Igluk Eskimos*, Copenhagen, 1929.

Rees, Alwyn and Brinley, *Celtic Heritage*, London, 1961.

Rhys, John, *Lectures on the Origin and Growth of Religion as Illustrated by Celtic Heathendom*, Hibbert Lectures, 1888.

Ross, Professor Anne, *Folklore of the Scottish Highlands*, London, 1976.

Ross, Professor Anne, *Pagan Celtic Britain*, London, 1974.

Sen, K M, *Hinduism*, Harmondsworth, 1975.

Shirokogoroff, S M, *Psychological Complex of the Tungus*, London, 1935.

Sjoestedt, M L, *Dieux et Heros de Celtes*, trs M Dillon, Paris, 1940.

Sjoestedt, M L, *Le Siege de Druim Damghaire*, Revue Celtique, XLIII, 1–123, 1926.

Soustelle, Jacques, *The Daily Life of the Aztecs*, Paris, 1955; London, 1961.

Stenning, E H, *A Portrait of the Isle of Man*, London, 1958.

Stokes, W, *Adventure of St Columba's Clerics*, Revue Celtique, XXVI; 130–92, 1905.

Stokes, W, *The Battle of Allen*, Revue Celtique, XXIV, 41–70, 1903.

Stokes, W, *The Battle of Mag Mucrime*, Revue Celtique, XIII, 426–74, 1892.

Stokes, W, *The Birth and Life of St Moling*, Revue Celtique, XXVII, 1906.

Stokes, W, *The Bodeleian Amra Cholimb Chille*, Revue Celtique, XX, 30, 132, 1248, 400, 1899.

Stokes, W, *Bruiden Da Chola* (Da Chola's Hostel), Revue Celtique, XXI, 149–65, 312–27, 388–402. 1900.

Stokes, W, *Coir Annan Irische Texte*, Leipzig, 1897.

Stokes, W, *The Destruction of Da Derga's Hostel*, Revue Celtique, XXII, 9, 165, 282, 390, 1901.

Stokes, W, *Find and the Phantoms*, Revue Celtique, VII, 389–307, 1886.

Stokes, W (and Windisch, E ed.), *The Irish Ordeals*, Irische Texte, Leipzig, 1891.

Stokes, W, *Life of St Fechin of Fore*, Revue Celtique, XII, 318–53, 1891.

Stokes, W, *Lives of the Saints from the Book of Lismore*, Oxford, 1890.

Stokes, W, *Prose Tales in the Rennes Dindshenchas*, Revue Celtique, XV, 272–336, 418–84. 1894.

Stokes, W, *The Rennes Dindshenchas*, Revue Celtique, XVI, 31–83, 1895.

Stokes, W, *Sanas Cormaic*, Calcutta, 1868.

Stokes, W, *The Second Battle of Moytura*, Revue Celtique XII, 52–130, 1891.

Stokes, W, *The Siege of Howth*, Revue Celtique, VIII, 47–64, 1887.

Stokes, W, *The Violent Deaths of Goll and Garb*, Revue Celtique, XIV, 396–449, 1893.

Stokes, W, *The Voyage of Hui Iorra*, Revue Celtique, 22–69, 1893.

Stokes, W, *The Voyage of Mael Phin*, Revue Celtique, IX, 447–95, 1888.

Stokes, W, *The Voyage of Snedgus and MacRiagla*, Revue Celtique, IX, 14–25, 1888.

Turville-Petre, E O G, *Myth and Religion of the North*, London, 1964.

Vendryes, J, *La Religion des Celtes*, Paris, 1948.

Vries, J de, *La Religion des Celtes*, Paris, 1963.

Weber, Max, *The Religion of India*, London, 1958.

Wright, R P, *The Whitley Castle Altar to Apollo*, Journal of the Royal Society, XXXIII, 36–8, 1943.

Index